JANICE ROSSER ALLEN
AND ELLEN VAUGHN

GOD IN THE CROSSROADS

Signs of Hope

surprising stories of grace from around the world

To the glory of God,

and dedicated to

Shirley Sutton Rosser,

a woman who has always devoted herself
to God and to her family,

and

Mildred Miller Santilli,

a woman who loved God's creative
work around the world.

TABLE OF CONTENTS

THE GOD WHO HUNG ON THE CROSS

ELLEN VAUGHN

That long-ago day in Cambodia I didn't know my life was about to change. I was just sure it was going to end.

I was flying—sort of—in a dilapidated, sputtering, Soviet-era helicopter with a nice man named Dois Rosser and a dozen other friends. We had wobbled into the air from a military runway in Phnom Penh and were now buzzing over flooded rice paddies, banana trees, and skeptical water buffalo. Due to abundant holes in the fuselage and the fact that the copter's rusty gas tank was surely going to explode, I surmised my days on earth would end somewhere above the jungle in Southeast Asia.

Dois Rosser, founder of International Cooperating Ministries, had hired me to write a book with and for him about ICM. My first—and I thought last—opportunity to see the ministry in action was during this trip to Cambodia.

To my surprise, International Cooperating Ministries would change—not end—my life.

The ministry exposed me to fresh, exotic, almost-unbelievable stories of hope and faith that I never knew existed, and the resulting book was published in 2003. Ever since then, readers from all over the world have let us know they loved its stories of God's transforming power in some of the worst places on the planet. Many told us how they had been challenged to trust God more, that their faith had grown, and that they had been moved to help poor and spiritually desperate people.

Many, many readers also urged us to write a sequel to that first book.

ICM's ministry, now in nearly 80 countries, has grown enormously since 2003. In this book, you will meet Christians from many of these places, particularly areas where believers are targets of persecution and discrimination. Their faith is New Testament faith: strong, creative, and culture-changing.

I sipped strong, bitter coffee one day with a courageous couple in a Muslim-majority nation where jihadists kill with impunity. "People have told us to leave our country, to get out to a safer place," they said. "But we cannot leave. Every day here, God is at work. People are coming to know Him, and embracing the way of love, rather than hate. God is doing what is humanly impossible!"

When I'm at home, sipping a sweet latte in the comfort of the U.S., I think of heroes like this. Their faith strengthens my faith and increases my vision of what God can do right here in America.

I hope your experience will be the same as you read this book. It's not a sequel to *The God Who Hung on the Cross*. Its personality and style are different, for I wrote it in partnership with my dear friend, Janice Allen. Janice is Dois Rosser's youngest daughter, and she has served as ICM's CEO since 2006. (I should note that at age 94, Dois is at the ICM office every day, still visionary, still advancing God's work around the world. I recently traveled with him to visit believers in a very violent country in Central America, and he was the most urgent, spiritually tireless person on that trip.)

The chapters that follow are written from Janice's perspective. They tell some of her personal story, blended with the broader story of ICM. Both narratives show God's amazing grace and faithfulness, particularly when hope seems lost. They offer a big takeaway for all of us, that even when events in our lives are just not going how we would choose, God really is at work. We can trust Him.

For friends who haven't read the first book, allow me to share one of its most dramatic accounts, one that shows this same truth. I heard this story on that long-ago day of my death-defying helicopter adventure, once I landed—alive— in a humid jungle in northern Cambodia.

In 1999, a pastor I'll call Tuy Seng traveled to a province in the northern part of Cambodia. Pastor Seng had wanted to bring the Gospel of hope to the villages in that part of his country for a long time, but the area had long been under the control of an isolated pocket of communist radicals who had killed many of his fellow citizens.

As far as anyone knew, Pastor Seng was the first person to speak of Jesus in that secluded part of Cambodia. Most villagers had followed Buddhism, ancestral worship, or animism for generations. Christianity was unheard of.

However, as Pastor Seng talked with the welcoming people in one community, they could not hear enough about Jesus. Most of the villagers decided, quickly, to follow Christ rather than the old ways.

Smiling, Pastor Seng asked the people why it seemed as if they had been waiting for him to come.

An old woman shuffled to the front of the group of people. She bowed, in the custom of her people, and grasped Pastor Seng's hands.

"We *have* been waiting," she said. "We have been waiting for you for 20 years."

Then she told him this story.

A notorious guerilla movement called the Khmer Rouge took over Cambodia after the Vietnam War, in the mid-1970s. The communists destroyed just about anything created with purpose and design—bridges, highways, hospitals . . . and human beings. It took a while for them to annihilate a fourth of the country's population, but after they had dealt with the capital and other city centers, they focused on the villages. They left killing fields full of human skulls wherever they went. Their atrocities eventually captured the attention of the civilized world, though, by then, it was too late for the millions who had died.

The communist soldiers came to this remote Cambodian hamlet in 1979. Their technique was the same as it had been for countless communities, but for the people who lived in this village, the terror was new. The soldiers emerged from the jungle and strode from hut to hut, ordering the villagers out. They killed any who resisted.

The rest of the people were marched to a clearing behind the community, forced to carry their farm tools with them.

"Dig!" the soldiers shouted.

The people hacked at the soil, trembling with the dark realization that they were digging their own mass grave. Some lost their nerve and tried to run. They were shot and dragged to the edge of the still-shallow pit.

Hours passed as the people sweated, wept, and dug. Finally, the hole was deep enough. The people laid down their spades and shovels. The soldiers shouted for them to turn and face the pit.

They braced themselves, waiting for the killing blows. They knew from stories that had come from other doomed villages that the soldiers would bludgeon them to death rather than shoot them all. Why waste bullets on ordinary peasants?

The heavy, humid air lay still as the villagers began to cry out. It was the wail before death, when the heart's longing to live becomes a desperate plea. Some screamed to Buddha, to ancestors, to demon spirits. Some cried out for their mothers.

Then one woman began to cry out, intuitively, to a figure in a story she had heard as a child. She didn't remember much, just that it was the story about a God who had hung on a cross. She called out to this God. Surely, the One who had suffered Himself might have compassion on those about to die.

Time stopped. The humid jungle air lay still.

Then the screams around the woman became a great wail, as the entire village called out, as one, crying for their lives, crying out to the God who hung on the cross, sobbing into the darkness of the pit before them.

There was only silence.

Silence.

Then, a flicker of hope.

Slowly, the people turned away from the pit, one by one.

The jungle was empty. The soldiers had fled.

And for 20 years, ever since that astounding day in 1979, the people of that village had been waiting . . . waiting for someone to come and tell them more, more about the God who hung on the cross, so they could know Him.

This account of the God who hung on the cross became a signature story for ICM many years ago. I now serve as the least-distinguished member of its board of directors, and we still hear these kinds of stories every day. They come from all over the world, from cruel and unlikely places. In spite of upheaval, war, and the advance of ISIS and other terrorist groups, there are powerful, joyous God stories that aren't often making it onto your newsfeeds or into the headlines. There is so much good news to know, so much real, substantive hope in this broken world today.

That's why we wrote this book!

Ellen Vaughn
25 February 2016
Washington, D.C.

PART 1

JANICE'S JOURNEY

CHAPTER 1

CONNECT THE DOTS

"I don't know what your destiny will be, but one thing I know:
the only ones among you who will be really happy
are those who have sought and found how to serve."
Albert Schweitzer

When I was a little girl, I loved playing "Connect the Dots." The game's pages looked like a formless, random sprinkling of dots, each one numbered. But, if you moved your pencil from dot one to two to three to four, a clear picture emerged from the disarray. Whoever designed the picture had predetermined the eventual, purposeful outcome. As a child, with my stubby pencil in hand, I trusted that the image would appear, even if the lines didn't seem to make sense. I just had to do my part to help make it happen.

3

It's a simplistic metaphor, but for me, it's always served as a powerful picture of God's purposeful design in my life. When I trust God, I know He is connecting me with people along the path, and He has a plan for the events of my life to ultimately accomplish His divine purpose. Sometimes those events feel random or way out of the bounds of how I think the picture should look. But I believe the Master Designer has a great plan. I'm a part of it, and I need to be willing to follow His lead. Sometimes I get to see the finished design; sometimes I don't. I do know that one day, I'll see the ultimate picture.

The connect-the-dot metaphor applies to ICM's ministry as well. Fittingly, the centerpiece of our office in Virginia is a large map of the world, covered with red dots. Each dot represents the GPS location where a church project now stands, built through the connections ICM has with our indigenous ministry partners and the U.S. donors who give funds to make those projects a reality.

At the beginning of 2016, ICM's map had 5,800 red dots in 78 countries.

We have a second map that layers black dots over the map with the red dots. The black dots each represent a daughter congregation that the ICM-sponsored mother church has planted. As I write, the 5,800 "red dot" mother congregations have planted more than 32,000 daughter congregations.

These maps aren't about objectives, plans, or statistics. They are about people. Each dot represents a congregation full of human beings whose lives have been touched and transformed by the power of God. Each dot is full of stories. Stories of congregations that prayed for years to have their own place to gather and worship. Stories of pastors in Tanzania who have faced death because of their refusal to deny Christ. Stories of widows in India who sacrificed their only inheritance, their ancestral land, in order to have a church. Stories of farmers in Vietnam willing to sell their only water buffalo and pull the plow themselves so they could give money to help build their church.

You will read some of these ICM stories in this book; there are so many more that we won't even know until we get to heaven. You'll also read about my own journey. I pray that God might use both—my story and ICM's broader narrative—to encourage you in your own journey with Him.

CHAPTER 2

URGENT TIMES

"When you find your definitions in God, you find the very purpose for which you were created. Put your hand into God's hand, know His absolutes, demonstrate His love, present His truth, and the message of redemption and transformation will take hold."

Ravi Zacharias

This is a story about hope and new beginnings. For some, a real sense of hope is tough to imagine.

Some of us have been bereaved, betrayed, and disappointed. Our situation feels wearisome or almost hopeless, as if we are stuck in an old rut we just cannot escape.

For others in far away places, a new beginning would be a miracle. People in difficult situations around the world desperately need a new start. Many live in the dust of poverty.

Many are minority groups, persecuted and hassled for their faith or ethnic origins, chased from their homes by terrorists, living in refugee camps. Many are women, seen as second-class citizens, disdained, abused, and sad. They, and their male counterparts, feel like they are at the absolute end of hope.

However, new beginnings are possible. When hope seems dead, it still exists.

I know this from unexpected disasters that thwarted my plans and broke my heart. I thought I was at the end of the road, but then I discovered that God had new plans for me, and in exploring them, I learned that He is far bigger, more loving, and more graciously surprising than I had imagined.

My experience of all this began with my father, Dois Rosser.

Dad is a very successful businessman and entrepreneur in the Tidewater area of Virginia. Back in his middle-age years, he was a leader in the community, in the commercial world, and in religious circles. He had known about Jesus all his life. Then Dad ran into an unconventional Bible teacher named Dick Woodward. Dick's insights about the Bible revolutionized Dad's faith, and the older Dad got, the more Jesus Christ intrigued him. Dad loved Christ's message of love and transformation. As a businessman, he thought of the Gospel as, among other things, the best product in the world.

Further, Dad had a strong understanding of the power and potential of local churches. He thought of them as God's own distribution system, designed to get the Good News about Christ to people in need. He wanted to figure out a way he could make it possible for more and more people in developing nations to benefit from the life-giving presence of local churches in their communities.

The result of Dad's dream was a charitable nonprofit called International Cooperating Ministries, or ICM. Dad founded ICM when he was 65, an age when most successful businesspeople like him were playing golf, sitting at the country club bar, and taking cruises to exotic ports of call.

Dad was traveling, too, but his destinations were less glamorous: leper congregations in the dusty villages of India, jungle huts in Vietnam, and slums in Central America. He developed partnerships with indigenous believers and helped them expand what they could do on their own. ICM provided money to help congregations build churches; the people provided the land and sweat equity, or labor, to build the buildings.

Dad also had a powerful resource to equip people with the life-changing truths of the Bible. This was Dick Woodward's unique overview of the Bible, improbably called the Mini Bible College, or MBC, though it was neither miniature nor a college.

So these two elements—nurturing believers in their faith and building churches—became the mission of International Cooperating Ministries, established in 1986.

The churches ICM builds are transformational forces in some of the most violent and challenging places on the planet. They are worship centers, community hubs, and places of refuge for abused women and children. They provide protection for those who are vulnerable to persecution and gang violence. They are vocational training centers, medical clinics, orphanages, and child-care facilities. They are the locus of solid biblical discipleship for growing Christian communities. They are places where people can come together, worship God, and build nourishing friendships as brothers and sisters in Christ.

By early 2016, ICM had worked, as we've said, in 78 countries and built 5,800 churches, orphanages, and centers for women, children, and young people. Indigenous believers had been involved in more than 170,000 Bible study classes, in 40 different languages. We had invested well more than $100 million in God's work around the world. Our Bible study tools—online, through solar-powered audio players, radio, and cell-phone chips—were reaching more than 275,000 people each year, most in very poor and persecuted places.

In the beginning, my father didn't have such a big, strategic plan for an international ministry. He was only one guy in Virginia with a bunch of like-minded friends. They were all just doing the next thing they believed God wanted them to do.

If Dad—the high-powered entrepreneur and businessman—was the last person you would expect to start a global Christian ministry, his self-effacing friend Dick Woodward was the last person you would expect to author a Bible overview that is reaching the world.

Dick was a gifted local pastor who was struck down by a mysterious disease at the height of his preaching ministry. He became a bedfast quadriplegic who could only move his head. He lay in a narrow hospital bed in his home in Williamsburg, Virginia, cared for by his loving family.

Dick's spirit was strong, even as his body was weak. He used a voice-activated computer as he refined the Mini Bible College and wrote books and other studies. For more than 20 years, this immobile man, whose physical body was wasting away, created a body of work that is now reaching people around the world. When grateful students would find out that the pastor behind this transformational teaching was a "helpless" quadriplegic, they were astonished. "If the Bible can give Pastor Dick hope," said one rural pastor in India, "God's Word can surely do the same for me."

Unlike Dick Woodward, I enjoyed great health, stamina, and a lifestyle that was comfortable in every way. Then God struck down my secure life and broke it into pieces. I didn't know how He was going to connect it all back together again, but He led me, to my surprise, to take on the leadership of ICM's ministry as CEO. There were plenty of places on that road where it would have been easy to detour, check out, or give up the journey. But there was always God's presence, beckoning on with a whisper of hope.

Because of my experience, I feel the solidarity of hope with others around the world.

I've worshipped with African sisters and brothers as they've danced and praised God in Swahili. I've wept as I've listened to Chinese, Vietnamese, and Cambodian Christians singing ancient hymns to the glory of God . . . or Colombian believers waving their hands in praise . . . or Christ-followers in the former Soviet Union rejoicing in open worship. I think of my suffering sisters and brothers in countries where Christians are persecuted by majority extremists, yet hold strong in their faith. I also think of former Muslims who now follow Jesus in countries where ICM is working, but cannot name, due to security issues.

When I worship God with my brothers and sisters from different cultures, I get a glimpse of what I will one day see in full reality, as is written in the biblical account in Revelation:

> . . . I looked, and there before me was a great multitude that no one could count, from every nation, tribe, people and language, standing before the throne and before the Lamb. They were wearing white robes and

*were holding palm branches in their hands. And they
cried out in a loud voice:*

> *'Salvation belongs to our God,*
> *who sits on the throne,*
> *and to the Lamb.'*[1]

This is the biblical vision of our future hope. ICM is committed to doing everything we can to help add millions to that eventual multitude.

The times have never been more urgent.

As I write, Christians are being sidelined, harassed, and slaughtered in the Middle East, North Africa, India, and many other places where ICM is active. Meanwhile, statisticians tell us that more than 2.6 billion people have never even heard the Good News about Jesus Christ.

Physical and educational needs are also daunting. More than 2.8 billion of the 7 billion people in the world live on less than $2's worth of food per day. Eight hundred million kids go to sleep hungry, every night. Nearly a billion people entered the twenty-first century unable to read a book or sign their own names. Almost 3.5 billion people live in villages lacking basic electricity and sewer services; most lack access to clean water.[2]

Many women in these settings routinely experience sexual and physical abuse; they have little recourse. Sex trafficking is rampant all over the world. Basic human rights are not so basic. In China, for example, in spite of the government's "generous" new two-child policy, couples must obtain a birth permit before conceiving . . . or face forced abortions.

At ICM, we feel that the best solution to physical, spiritual, and relational human problems is to unleash the capability of the local indigenous church. We believe that the Church Jesus established is His plan for cultural change. From its beginnings in the book of Acts to its many expressions in the world today, the local church channels the transformational power of God's love.

If villagers need clean water, believers dig the well. If malaria is threatening the community, the church connects with medical groups that provide mosquito netting. Believers protect children and women from those who would abduct or abuse them. These outreaches—much like the "social work" of the first-century church—draw people in to experience the love of Jesus, expressed through His people. The Holy Spirit frees people from ancestor worship or devotion to trees, stones, or idols. They learn how to live at peace with one another, to respect one another in love. They become full of hope, despite their difficult circumstances.

I've seen this in some pretty hopeless places.

CHAPTER 3

THE DOOR
OF HOPE

"Hope is the very dynamic of history. Hope is the engine of change. Hope is the energy of transformation . . . Things that seem possible, reasonable, understandable, even logical in hind-sight . . . often seemed quite impossible, unreasonable, nonsensical, and illogical when we were looking ahead to them . . .

"Between impossibility and possibility, there is a door, the door of hope. And the possibility of history's transformation lies through that door . . . Spiritual visionaries have often been the first to walk through that door, because in order to walk through it, first, you have to see it, and then, you have to believe that something lies on the other side."

Diana Butler Bass

I recently met a young woman in Honduras, one of the most violent countries in the world. I will call this woman Sonya.

Sonya was in a wheelchair. When I met her, she was singing and praising God in a vibrant little church that ICM had built. One night, she and her husband had been walking down a road in their village, and a gang of young men surrounded them. They hacked her husband to death with machetes, right in front of her. As she wept and pleaded, they cut off both of her arms and left her to die a slow, painful death.

A church member found her, bleeding out on the road. He picked her up, took her for medical care, and brought her to his family. In Honduras, there aren't any government disability programs providing a safety net. If you cannot use your hands to work, you can't buy food or shelter. Sonya couldn't even feed herself. If not for the constant care of the Christian community, she would be dead or on the street, begging for food.

In every way, the community of believers in Jesus has saved this young woman's life. Her church family feeds her, takes care of her, and she has dignity, and even joy, because of the people of God.

Though there is little to tie me, in a worldly sense, to this armless sister in Honduras, our convictions about the future are the same. Our certainties are the same. Our hope is ultimately the same.

In my work as a clinical oncology nurse in the 1980s, I founded a home-care hospice program in Florida and later worked with cancer patients receiving treatment in research protocols. I had no way of knowing that cancer would be part of my own story, much later, but my courageous patients and their families constantly inspired me. One of the most powerful lessons they taught me had to do with the nature of hope.

When someone is first diagnosed with cancer, he or she hopes that it won't be a bad kind with a poor prognosis, or they hope that the tumor is contained and easily removable. People facing surgery, chemotherapy, or radiation hope that their treatments will eradicate the disease so they can move on with life. When I was a nurse for new research protocols, patients for whom every other treatment had failed hoped that this new one would succeed and their cancer would finally be vanquished.

When patients moved to hospice, I saw that their hope had changed. But it was still there. *I hope I can make it to Christmas. I hope my family will be with me. I hope I won't have pain. I hope I can die with dignity.*

Hope is fundamental to the human spirit. When people—either ill or healthy—lose all hope, they die inside. Some follow through and die physically as well, taking their own lives.

Having watched the slippery slope of hope with so many brave patients, I've returned again and again to the power of the Gospel message. God designed us, as human beings, to be predisposed to hope. And when we come to the end, as believers, when there is logically no more hope to be had, that's when the most profound hope eclipses everything else. It is our firm hope for life in eternity with Christ that takes away the cold fear that death is the end.

I've not only seen this in people dying of cancer, but in the lives of persecuted Christians suffering in prison, as well as in women whose days are full of hard labor and whose nights are dark with abuse, in believers in Jesus whose homes and churches are burned by terrorists. When hope in any human possibility of change is gone, God still gives the eternal flame of His promises.

For me, the journey to this kind of radical hope began in a conventional setting.

I had the quintessential childhood of 1950s and '60s America. My parents, part of the "greatest generation," were hardworking, God-fearing folks whose own parents had worked in blue-collar jobs, wore hand-me-downs, and grew their own food. My childhood weekend highlights included root beer floats with my Meme and Pop-pop. Evenings flowed with singalongs, Ping-Pong in the carport, and kick-the-can after the sun went down.

Faith in God was the backbone of our family for generations. Our first paternal ancestor, John Rosser, arrived in the U.S. from Wales around 1750. Following in his footsteps, the rest of the Rossers were all in churches—both Presbyterian and Baptist—every Sunday.

The notion of missions was important in both denominations. At the Baptist church, I heard all about the Southern Baptist missionary, Lottie Moon, who worked in China from 1873 to 1940. In a time when women weren't always recognized, she almost singlehandedly laid a foundation for U.S. Baptists' understanding of worldwide missions. This captured my imagination.

Meanwhile, in the Presbyterian Church, I was deeply touched by our pastor's wife, who had grown up in China as a missionary's daughter.

Sandy Mallinson was the closest thing to an angel I knew. She modeled Christ's joy and sacrificial love in every way. Living on her pastor husband's small salary, she raised a houseful of kids, and she loved the rest of us who were not her biological children. I remember many Sunday afternoon lunches of pea soup, games, and lots of love.

Our little church always had missionary speakers and international visitors. Bob Daly was a mail carrier in our congregation, and each Sunday morning, he would go to Hampton Harbor, where international ships docked from all over the world. Bob would talk with sailors who were wandering about onshore and bring any who were interested to our church and lunch afterward.

I remember the stories of another visitor, not a sailor, but a pastor named Burt Reed who served with Trans World Radio. As a little girl, I'd sit at the kitchen table, enthralled by Burt's tales of what God was doing in distant parts of the world, dreaming about helping people in faraway lands. Burt would become one of my dad's closest friends and his first associate at International Cooperating Ministries. Now in his eighties, Burt still serves full-time in the ministry, his office just around the corner from mine.

Working hard and sacrificing much was a part of my parents' fiber. Their marriage was a typical 1950s-style union. Dad was the provider and handled all the finances; Mom managed the household and the child rearing. She deferred to Dad in most things.

Instead of going to college, my father had used his GI Bill money after World War II to build some modest houses in Virginia's Tidewater area. He sold them so he could build some more . . . the intuitive beginnings of his leveraging of resources that would shape ICM's ministry many years later.

My father worked from 7 a.m. to 7 p.m., Monday through Saturday. He started real estate endeavors, a car dealership, and all kinds of other businesses. He was constantly meeting with people or on the phone, working one aspect or another of his various businesses. He often didn't know how he would make payroll.

Before I was born, my mother went to the hospital to deliver my sister, Cindy. It was December 22. Meanwhile, my dad was hours away, driving to his car dealership. He had scratched together enough money to pay his employees, so they could buy Christmas gifts for their families.

Mom, a hero, delivered alone. Cindy arrived. And my dad delivered checks to his employees.

Throughout their marriage, my mother sacrificed to enable my father to do what he did so well. By the time they were retirement age, they were quite comfortable, financially, but their lifestyle didn't change much. They poured their resources into Dad's new enterprise, ICM, and Mom's retirement travel meant going with my father on long flights and even longer bus rides over bumpy dirt roads to visit congregations in poor villages all over India. Not exactly Club Med. She smiled, packed a small suitcase, and went with him everywhere.

My mother modeled unreserved love. She was always available to listen and provide wise advice and warm hugs. She showed me the God of unconditional love. She created a home full of love, security, joy, and peace.

My father?

Dad was driven, creative, and gifted in business with an uncanny ability to understand leveraging, management of cash flow, and finances. His mind is an incredible calculator; even in his mid-90s, he can beat most computers to arrive at a mathematically sound solution to any problem. I learned from him about commitment, focus, and the importance of being a person of truth and integrity. He created an atmosphere that valued performance, achievement, and independence.

My oldest sister, Pam, was the high-energy, social butterfly of the household. She was popular, the perfect cheerleader, and just enough older than me that I would dream about one day wearing her clothes and having boyfriends, too. To this day, Pam can energize a room; she is hilarious and has intuitive nurturing skills with people, particularly small children, as she worked for 30 years as a kindergarten teacher.

My next sister, Cindy, was 18 months older than me and just 1 year ahead in school. She excelled in everything. For sisters whose father had high expectations, we faced years of sibling rivalry, but we ended up as true friends and soul mates. Cindy became an ordained Presbyterian minister. She has a great vision for the transformational power of a local church and the richness of corporate worship.

As the youngest daughter, I felt challenged to balance the high-achievement values and the need to be in control with the Christian directive to trust God in all things and wait for Him to move. I wanted to be a high achiever like my dad. I also wanted to be a nurturing, sacrificial person like my mom. I wanted it all.

My faith blended with the notion that I could somehow achieve joy and purpose through my own hard efforts. The better I did in school, at work, or in other challenges, and the better I performed in Christian disciplines, the better life would be.

It's unfortunately easy, particularly in comfortable America, to combine Christianity with cultural values of success, performance, and appearances. That false mind-set creates a tremendous amount of pressure. Faith can become a self-sufficient gospel that is long on human control and short on surrender to Jesus.

None of this false theology was my parents' intention for me. They modeled a beautiful sense of Christian dependence on God, love, and hospitality. My father would take me along when he delivered turkeys at Thanksgiving to people in need. I would see him quietly deliver groceries, or surreptitiously help with a mortgage payment when someone was in a tough place. My mother volunteered at a crisis-counseling center to offer a word of comfort or prayer to someone in an emergency. Mom and Dad gave anonymously, spontaneously, and generously. They believed that their money belonged to God. They were just stewards of it.

Given my upbringing, the issue of Christian faith was not even a question. I had always known about Jesus.

It's one thing to recognize that Christianity is true in your head. It's another thing to know Jesus in your *heart*. For me, that reality took a little bit longer to come true.

I was like a marlin, that blue, deep-sea fish that battles fishermen.

My dad taught me that deep-sea fishing is an art. First, you must hook the fish using the right bait and the correct hook and line. You must give the fish plenty of line to run, or else the line will break as the fish fights. Whenever the fish surfaces and comes closer, you slowly reel in more line, drawing the fish ever closer to the fisherman, the one in control. It can be a very long, drawn-out process, but the angler's patience endures as the fish runs away repeatedly, and gradually comes closer.

And closer.

Even as a young person, I always felt hooked by God. I was stubborn and ran out my line quite a bit. Though I knew better, I felt like Christianity was a bunch of rules and regulations. I questioned God deeply when one of my friends committed suicide. But God had me . . . and gently, gradually, He drew me in.

The devotional writer Oswald Chambers may not have known much about deep-sea fishing; he surely didn't know or care that I happened to be a marlin. But I love what he wrote about the process of God pulling us into Himself:

> *Being born again by the Spirit is an unmistakable work of God, as mysterious as the wind, and as surprising as God Himself. We don't know where it begins—it is hidden away in the depths of our soul. Being born again from above is an enduring, perpetual, and eternal beginning. It provides a freshness all the time in thinking, talking, and living—a continual surprise of the life of God.*[3]

So, yes, by God's grace, I was born again. But I still struggled with classic questions of identity. Who was I, really, and what role did God have for me?

CHAPTER 4

HALT! HUNGRY, ANGRY, LONELY, AND TIRED

"The aim of Satanic power is to cut off
communication with God.
To accomplish this aim he deludes the soul with
a sense of defeat, covers him with a thick cloud of darkness,
depresses and oppresses the spirit,
which in turn hinders prayer and leads to
unbelief—thus destroying all power."
                                        James O. Fraser

When I was in middle school, I happened on a book by Dr. Albert Schweitzer, the German theologian who became a medical missionary to Africa in the early 1900s.

I was touched by his practical demonstrations of God's love as he met the people's needs in a land so different from anything I had ever known.

Dr. Schweitzer's story planted the seed for missions in my heart. His humanitarian adventures captured my imagination. *When I grow up,* I thought, *I want to do the same. I want to help people who are in physical and spiritual pain.* My dream was to one day go to nursing school and become a medical missionary in some exotic foreign setting.

You know how it is with childhood dreams. Sometimes we forget them and pursue other things. Sometimes our dreams get lost in the unexpected storms or choppy tides of life.

I did go into nursing, and went to college and graduate school during the height of the women's movement. There was a lot of talk back then about breaking glass ceilings in careers. Many 1970s students looked at the 1950s model and went to its opposite extreme. There was a lot of "I am woman, hear me roar" rhetoric in dorm discussions, and a lot of shared female rage. Some of my peers felt repressed and denied, and they were mad.

I had chosen a traditionally female profession, but was part of the first generation of nurses who were moving into expanded careers as clinical specialists and nurse practitioners. I wasn't angry or on the women's liberation bandwagon of the day, but I didn't want the typical female role of my parents' generation, either. I wanted a successful career as an oncology nurse and nurse educator.

I also wanted to fall in love and get married, but I didn't want to repeat my parents' model of marriage. I dreamed of a marriage where roles were not automatically prescribed. I longed for a marriage where spouses would encourage one another to maximize gifts and talents, and each would be willing to share in child rearing and household responsibilities.

Today, that doesn't sound very radical, but 4 decades ago was a time of transition. I didn't want the 1950s' options I'd seen growing up, nor did I want the angry feminism of the '70s.

I met Bob Allen on a date set up by mutual friends when he was in medical school and I was in nursing school at the University of Virginia. Ironic: the budding ophthalmologist met his future wife on a blind date. After that first evening, it seemed we were constantly running into each other around the hospital or eating sandwiches on the steps in front of the medical school.

Romance for healthcare providers can have its own set of challenges. At Bob's apartment, while looking for hors d'oeuvres, I grabbed a jar of large olives in the refrigerator —only to realize that, in fact, these were *not* olives, but *cow eyeballs* to be used for research. And Bob would write me love letters on patient history forms when he was on call in the middle of the night.

So romantic.

I got pregnant one month after we were married. I had finished graduate school just before the wedding and was only weeks into my "perfect" job. Bob was 3 months into his ophthalmology residency at the University of Florida.

Life changed. No more love letters or jokes about medical appetizers. Bob was driven, talented, and sprinting down his career track. I was at home with a son in diapers. My nursing training, my master's degree from Duke University, and all the academic achievements I had enjoyed were now usurped by a life of baby bottles and plastic toddler toys scattered all over the living-room floor. Bob was gone long hours and usually arrived home ready to collapse in bed, exhausted. He came home, unfortunately, to a wife who was hungry for attention, angry, lonely, and tired.

Over the next couple of years, our marriage weakened under these stresses, as well as unexpressed bitterness. When Bob accepted a 2-year research fellowship at Massachusetts Eye and Ear Infirmary in Boston, we considered the possibility of my staying behind and ending our marriage.

This was not the life story I had hoped for.

I did go to Boston with Bob. We got into marriage counseling. My mother encouraged me to become involved with Community Bible Study, a gathering of women who studied the scriptures together in small groups every week. We had daily homework and Bible verses to memorize. Our teaching director, Ginny Viola, was married to a doctor; she took me under her wing. She wisely let me know that in spite of all my best efforts and chiding, I really could not change my husband in an attempt to improve our marriage. She said, "Janice, the only person you can change is yourself. What you are responsible for is who you are in your relationship with God. That's the part you must work on."

I'm so grateful God put Ginny in my life! I was working part-time on the faculty of Boston University and doing a lot of ever-so-slightly resentful parenting because of Bob's demanding schedule. I wanted him to be the spiritual leader in our marriage, but at that point, I was the one who had more time for Bible study, fellowship with other believers, and reflection. I slowly began to realize that I was often sounding judgmental and preachy to my husband. I began to make decisions in a way consciously designed to preserve and restore my marriage, and to change me, from the inside out.

Our counselor told us to identify activities we enjoyed doing together, and so we soon embarked on a short-term medical mission trip to Nicaragua, the first of many. As I assisted Bob in eye surgeries in primitive conditions, *we* were the ones whose vision was healed. We began to see each other differently, as partners rather than competitors.

Meanwhile, our marriage counselor was also holding each of us accountable for working to communicate better. Though our lives were still hectic—with two more moves and two more baby boys—we made time for date nights. We focused more on the good qualities in each other and criticized less. And, as the years went by, thankfully, our sons never knew we'd gone through this rough season in our marriage—until they read the manuscript for this book!

CHAPTER 5

HUMAN DOINGS

*"An easy-going, non-self-denying life will never
be one of power."*

Hudson Taylor

Over the years, though, Bob's focus remained on his patients and his developing career. He made it a practice to go beyond the call of duty for his patients.

One such patient was Ethel, a spunky, tiny lady with silver hair. Her husband had died years earlier, and her children lived far away. The main love of her life was her small white dog, which actually looked quite a bit like her. Ethel was very worried about little Fifi, who had cataracts in both eyes, and thus, spent a lot of her time running into walls, tripping over rugs, and bumping into chairs.

Bob listened sympathetically as Ethel shared Fifi's myopic troubles. This was in the early 1980s, when laser surgery was a new procedure, even for humans, and very few veterinarians were offering it for their canine patients. Bob knew that Ethel didn't have much money for her own needs, let alone Fifi's cataracts. So, yes, he offered to operate on the dog.

The only problem was that doing this was just ever-so-slightly—well, totally—against normal hospital procedures.

So, one dark and stormy night, my tall, white-coated husband smuggled little Fifi into his hospital, with Ethel following in his wake. Praying that Fifi would not bark, burp, or whine, he placed the pooch in his medical bag. With Ethel trailing behind him, Bob crept up the back stairs to the fourth floor, an in-patient unit where the optical laser was located.

Bob made it safely to the deserted laser suite. He quickly anesthetized the dog, though not without some trepidation. He just didn't know quite how much anesthesia to administer for such a small animal.

Fifi commenced snoozing. Bob commenced operating. All was going quite well, and he had almost finished on the second eye, when Fifi started to wake up. Not enough anesthesia!

"Nice doggy! Nice doggy! Shhh!" whispered my frantic husband.

Fifi was having none of it. "*Yip, yip!*" she barked . . . over and over and over. Ethel stood at the head of the gurney, wringing her hands. Surely all was lost.

Bob quickly administered a bit more anesthesia, finished the procedure, and instructed Ethel to take sleeping Fifi down the back stairs. He threw the surgical sheets away and flung the instruments into a bin. Then he crossed his arms and began whistling softly, just as the front door swung open and Nurse Ratchet, head administrator of the floor, strode in.

She did not greet Bob, but cut right to the chase. "Did I hear barking in here?"

"Barking?" he asked innocently. "Why would there be barking?" He paused. "Oh, I know what you mean. The patient in the next room had the television turned up really loud a minute ago. You must have heard a dog on the TV."

She eyed him suspiciously, raised her eyebrows, and swept out of the room.

There were happy endings all around. Fifi could see, Ethel was thrilled, and fortunately, Bob did not lose his hospital privileges or his job.

As the years went by and our sons grew older, I began to notice that something strange was happening to my parents.

My dad had gotten a God-sized bee in his bonnet. He started traveling to India regularly and giving money to build churches in poor villages. As he saw the impact of these growing congregations, his business mind figured out how to multiply his efforts. He arranged for his friend Dick Woodward's transformational Bible teaching to become available in Indian languages. He partnered with indigenous leaders. He continued to replicate his discipleship training and church-building model all over the world. He got friends to see his vision . . . and gradually, bit by bit, International Cooperating Ministries was born.

My parents had always been generous and mission-minded. But I had not expected my dad to launch a new charitable organization in his mid-60s. I didn't expect my mom to jump on planes and rickshaws and donkey carts to accompany him on adventures off in the wild blue yonder.

My sisters and I saw, however, that this new initiative was exhilarating for our parents. It was making a huge difference in people's lives. Though we were busy with our own families, we solidly supported what Dad and Mom were doing.

So it was that we found ourselves in a family meeting on a beautiful weekend in April 1993. Dad and Mom had invited my two sisters, me, and our husbands, to the Homestead, a resort in Virginia's Blue Ridge Mountains.

On Saturday morning, we gathered for brunch. Dad, who was never nervous, seemed to be fumbling for words as he explained why he'd brought us here. He beat around several bushes, took a few U-turns, and finally spat it out. He and Mom were thinking about taking their entire estate and putting it into a foundation that would allow International Cooperating Ministries to serve people around the world for years to come.

The bottom line was this: how might we feel about our inheritance not coming to us, but going to ministry?

Two things happened.

First, my sisters and I were rather surprised at the amount of money Dad was talking about. We had grown up modestly, and I guess we hadn't been paying attention to the fact that our parents' nest egg had somehow grown sizably since our childhood.

Second, we didn't hesitate. We knew that ICM's ministry was helping people not just in this life, but for eternity. We had never spent time sitting around contemplating our parents' estate. We were all surprised that they were even asking about it. The inheritance wasn't *our* money. It was God's.

"Of course!" we all said, smiling. Our poor parents looked incredibly relieved . . . and there was laughter, tears, and whooping around the table.

Over the years, we had all traveled with ICM to remote places. We helped with the ministry, served on the board of directors, got our friends involved, and loved seeing how Dad's original ideas were growing into something substantial that would last for future generations, both in our family and in families around the world.

So, yes, we were totally on board with "our" inheritance being used to leverage and grow the ministry. We'd known for a long time that this would be our family's lasting legacy.

While my father's new ministry was in full swing, Bob continued climbing the ladder of success. He had trained at many of the best institutions—Duke, UVA, Johns Hopkins, and Harvard Medical School. His eyes were always on the next thing, straining for the next prize: the next research paper, the next speaking engagement, the next professorship. In 1994, he reached the height of his career when he became chairman of ophthalmology at Virginia Commonwealth University's School of Medicine.

In hindsight, Bob would later say that during this period, he felt like more of a "human doing" than a "human being." He was constantly in a hurry, always pressed. There was always just one more patient to see, one more appointment, and one more accomplishment.

As we settled into our lives in Richmond, Virginia, I compensated for his busyness by becoming equally busy with my own endeavors. Besides managing the household, I took on leadership roles in our church, women's Bible studies, and our local Young Life Committee, as well as greater responsibilities on ICM's board. (Little did I know that God was preparing me for my future role with ICM, still years down the road.)

The inner struggle I'd felt for years about advancing my own nursing career and developing my résumé was a vague memory. I felt fulfilled in doing for others.

Bob and I knew we were blessed in so many ways. We had all the things that mainstream culture—and some Christians—herald as marks of prosperity, success, and favor. It felt like everything was almost perfect.

Then something happened that didn't feel perfect at all.

CHAPTER 6

THE CLUB NO ONE
WANTS TO JOIN

*"I have learned to love the darkness of sorrow, for it is
there I see the brightness of God's face."*
Madame Guyon

It was just after the turn of the millennium, January 8,
2000. We had survived predictions that the world would
end when computers around the globe shut down for Y2K.
Bob was 49, and I was a few years younger. Our oldest son
Grant was in his last year of college; Matt was a junior in high
school; and Connor was in middle school.

It was a sunny Saturday, and Connor and I had driven to
Charlottesville from Richmond for a UVA basketball game.
Bob had spent the day at his office interviewing applicants

for an ophthalmology residency. His vision had been slightly fuzzy for a few days. Assuming he just needed new glasses, he asked a faculty member to examine him. They ran an ultrasound.

Though Bob's vision was blurred, the diagnosis was clear. There was a tumor hiding in his right eye. It had gotten so large that it was pulling on his retina.

Bob and his colleagues were sure it was ocular melanoma, a rare, aggressive, malignant cancer. They knew that the statistics were not in his favor. Fifty percent of ocular melanoma patients are dead in 3 years. If it spreads, or metastasizes, to other areas of the body, it is universally fatal.

When I arrived home that evening from the basketball game, Connor and I wanted to give Bob all the details of UVA's victory, but he was preoccupied. After the chatter calmed down and Connor left to play video games, Bob took me into our bedroom and sat me down in a chair, holding my hands.

"I have a tumor in my eye," he said simply. "I'm pretty sure it's ocular melanoma."

All I knew was that this was very bad. Bob calmly began to tell me about ocular melanoma, almost as if he was the doctor giving bad news to his patient.

I clung to my husband. Before that moment, life had been rolling out in calendar days, anniversaries, birthdays, and other events. For me, in that moment in my bedroom, looking into my husband's green eyes, it all stopped.

As a cancer nurse, I knew we were now in the realm where the days were measured by appointments with specialists, scans, and increasingly dire medical reports. I had worked with hundreds of patients with skin melanoma. I've had it myself. But I was completely unfamiliar and ill-prepared for ocular melanoma, with its poor prognosis, few known treatments, and no known cure.

The next morning, I left for church, leaving Bob at home to make phone calls to eye tumor specialists. During the worship service, I sat numb and confused. Where was God when cancer showed up and your life flipped upside down?

I held my emotions at bay until the final hymn, "Great Is Thy Faithfulness," and then I could not stop weeping. This would be the song that God would use repeatedly over the next 5 years, always at the exact time I needed it most, to remind me of His presence and care.

By Monday morning, less than 48 hours after Bob and his partner found his problem, we were at the Wills Eye Institute in Philadelphia. The specialists confirmed that it was indeed ocular melanoma, so we were now part of a very small community of people with this diagnosis. This was not a club I wanted to join.

The doctors recommended immediate removal of the eye. At our request, they delayed the surgery by 1 day so we could connect with our sons and family. You spend your entire parental life trying to protect your children from pain, and now, here we were, inflicting pain on them due to a situation beyond our control.

Even as the nurses prepared to take Bob to the operating room, I prayed for miraculous healing. Still hopeful, I asked the surgeon to please check the eye one more time before it was cut out to see if the tumor had miraculously disappeared.

It had not.

The surgeon removed Bob's right eye, his dominant eye. So my husband, the acclaimed ophthalmic microsurgeon, no longer had depth perception. The doctor whose passion it had been to save vision in others would never operate again.

For two triple-A personalities, this loss of capacity and control was very disconcerting. Later, we would joke, darkly, that it was ironic that Bob, the surgical ophthalmologist, and Janice, the oncology nurse, were facing life-threatening eye cancer. Why couldn't we have gone into pediatrics and obstetrics or something more benign?

The point is, we were healthcare specialists in the exact fields in which my husband was threatened, and we did not know what we were doing or where we were going.

The author of the devotional book, *Streams in the Desert*, says that the great patriarch of the Jews, Abraham, had the same challenge.

> *Abraham 'did not know where he was going'—it simply was enough for him to know he went with God. He did not lean as much on the promises as he did on the Promiser. O glorious faith! Your works and possibilities are these: contentment to set sail with the orders still sealed, due to unwavering confidence in the wisdom of the Lord High Admiral; and a willingness to get up, leave everything, and follow Christ, because of the joyful assurance that earth's best does not compare with heaven's least. You must be willing to take your ideas of what the journey will be like and tear them into tiny pieces, for nothing on the itinerary will happen as you expect.*[4]

With Bob's malignant cancer diagnosis, I could almost see the plans I'd had for our lives torn into tiny pieces, blowing away in a cold and frightening wind.

CHAPTER 7

THE GRACE YEARS

"Hope is not logical. It always comes as a surprise,
just when you think all hope is lost.
Hope is the cousin to grief, and both take time: you can't short-circuit
grief, or emptiness, and you can't patch it up with your bicycle tire
tube kit. You have to take the next right action. Things get broken—
they always do—and children yap and stamp and cry and demand
your attention. It's called real life, and it's cracked and fragile, but the
glue for me is the beating of my heart, love, and whatever attention
I can pay to what matters most to me . . . and the faith that
everyone—everyone—eventually falls into the hands of God.
Hope always catches us by surprise."

Anne Lamott

After Bob's diagnosis, his training as a medical researcher
kicked into gear. At that time, there was a void of easily
available information about ocular melanoma. It was very

difficult for most people to get data in order to make wise decisions about clinical protocols. Genetic markers and targeted cancer therapies were unheard of, so Bob's goal was to learn all he could about the latest research protocols across the country. He knew that unless there was a miracle, his own life would not be saved. But he wanted to research as much as he could in the hope that others with this disease might benefit in the future.

During this time, I served at ICM as vice chair of the board and helped the ministry with fund development. Though Bob could no longer operate on others, he continued his research and work at the hospital. We tried to be normal. Before we would go to a dinner party, Bob would have me check his eye to make sure his prosthesis was in right. And I was able to travel a bit. I went to Cambodia with Dad and our son Grant, who had graduated from college about 2 years earlier.

But in the spring of 2003, we got the news we knew was coming but still could not fathom: Bob's cancer had metastasized. There were now small tumors in his liver. Bob immediately sought out research protocols with a vague hope of slowing down the cancer's progression, but it continued to spread and grow.

We decided to make a last attempt to impede the growth of the tumors in Bob's liver and went to the National Institutes of Health in Maryland. Bob endured aggressive chemotherapy on a research protocol. NIH felt massive, cold, and sterile. It is an impressive bastion of research and science, and we were glad to be there, but it also felt far from the warmth and love of family and friends.

Our son Grant was working in nearby Washington, D.C., so he could visit in the evenings. It broke my heart to watch him try to come to terms with the fact that his once-invincible father was now a fragile cancer patient. Matt was entrenched in his premed studies at the University of Virginia, wishing he could somehow help. We had sent our youngest son, Connor, off to college just weeks before. It was so hard to tell Connor that his dad was in too much pain to go with us to get him settled at Duke, Bob's alma mater. I ached for my three sons.

As I walked the halls of this unfamiliar hospital, missing home, I paused to read the stitching on a handmade quilt, sewn by other patients, hanging on the wall. One square read, "Sometimes God calms the storm. Sometimes God calms His servant while the storm rages on." The storm of cancer was raging, but God was showing His care and love for us in the midst of it all.

On our twenty-seventh wedding anniversary, September 10, I sat near Bob's hospital bed at NIH, legs propped up, my feet touching his. I marveled over what God had done in our relationship. The level of intimacy and love between us had never been stronger. Bob's spirit toward me was so soft, loving, and grateful. God had healed the years of anger and resentment.

The cancer storm was raging on, but God filled us with an amazing sense of peace. It was a season of grace we'd never known before.

We returned home from NIH, only to find that toxic doses of Bob's chemotherapy had leaked systemically, resulting in life-threatening low blood counts and an emergency hospitalization for transfusions. These frequent, critical transfusions eventually resulted in frightening immune responses that brought extremely high fevers, trouble breathing, and extensive swelling.

The only solution was transfusing Bob with genetically similar, matched platelets. Most likely, this platelet donation would need to come from one or both of his biological brothers, Scott and Richard. After testing, we were hugely disappointed to discover that neither matched. We pled with the blood bank to test our two accessible sons, Connor and Matt. (Grant was traveling for work, and unavailable.)

Shocking the professionals, it turned out that both boys were matches. The hospital staff said it was a miracle. I knew it was an answer to our prayers. Our sons' platelets had the potential to save their father from a fatal hemorrhage.

Connor was a healthy 18-year-old, 6 feet 5 inches tall. He was 1 month into his first year of college. He'd never been in the hospital or had surgery of any kind. He grinned as he showed up at the Richmond blood bank, and then blanched a bit as the nurse stuck a large bore needle into his arm repeatedly before he finally found the vein. But Connor didn't falter. This was a gift he could give his dad.

Moments later, a local television news crew arrived. They were doing a story on the shortage of blood at the blood bank. When they interviewed me, I felt compelled to say a few words about our story—not only because my husband had probably helped cause the shortage—but also because giving blood saves lives.

Later that night, I returned to Bob's hospital room. I sat with him as we clicked on the 11 o'clock news. Weak and sick in his hospital bed, he watched his son with arm outstretched, giving blood so his father might be saved. Bob could not stop weeping.

This may not be great theology, but I saw a spiritual parallel. I had often considered the anguish Christ experienced in His brutal death on the cross. But I had never truly considered the pain and heartache of God the Father as He watched His only Son bleed and die on the cross. The Father and the Son both knew this sacrifice must be made to redeem the world into a right relationship with a holy God. A blood sacrifice had been made, and Christ came to earth to fulfill that assignment.

That night, in Bob's hospital room, it hit me how God's heart must have broken when He watched His beloved Son suffer and die. I sensed that God's heart was so tender for my family's pain, and I clung to the promise that God knew and held all my tears. I felt His loving Spirit envelop me.

Two days later, Bob was transfused with Connor's blood platelets, which we had started calling "liquid gold." The following day, Matt went to the lab near UVA and gave his blood. The packets were delivered to Richmond . . . and our sons' platelets gave Bob elevated levels of what was good, protected him from what was bad, and restored their father's bone marrow.

Their gift gave doctors valuable research information for other patients. And it gave Bob a little more time. Because of his sons' sacrifice, he lived 5 more precious months.

CHAPTER 8

WHITE STONE

"Almighty and eternal God,
Thou art hidden from my sight; Thou art beyond
the understanding of my mind; Thy thoughts are not my
thoughts; Thy ways are past finding out.
"Yet hast Thou breathed Thy Spirit into my life; Yet hast Thou
formed my mind to seek Thee; Yet hast Thou inclined my heart
to love Thee; Yet hast Thou made me restless for the rest that is
in Thee; Yet hast Thou planted within me a hunger and thirst
that make me dissatisfied with all the joys of earth.
"O Lord God, I praise and magnify Thy name that thus
Thou hast set Thy seal upon my inmost being . . . I bless Thee
for Thy hand upon my life, and for the sure knowledge that,
however I may falter and fail, yet underneath are
Thine everlasting arms. Amen."
John Baillie

By Christmas 2004, Bob's cancer had spread into his liver, lungs, bones, and lymph nodes. He was on strong narcotics for the pain. Just before the holidays, he had surgery on a large tumor in his neck, an area he referred to as "high-priced real estate."

The surgeon was a friend. In the waiting room he took me aside to say, "I wouldn't have done it for anyone else. Not much was gained except Bob's peace of mind. A lot of cancer is still there." I had often seen denial kick in when I was caring for cancer patients and their families. Now, I found it very difficult to face the stark truth as the surgeon's blunt words sunk in. I could no longer deny that, barring some miracle, my husband was going to die soon.

The American poet Ralph Waldo Emerson wrote that "Rings and jewels are not gifts, but apologies for gifts. The only true gift is a portion of thyself." True. But that Christmas, I also saw the gift of time. I saw how it gave us more of a portion of Bob himself.

After the holidays, our days were filled with doctor appointments, radiation treatments, and pain medications.

Just after Valentine's Day, Bob and I made his last trip to the little retirement home we had bought after his diagnosis, when we stopped postponing our dreams. We had wondered for some time what to name it. Now it became clear to us.

Revelation 2:17 says, "to him who overcomes, I will give some of the hidden manna. I will also give him a white stone with a new name written on it, known only to him who receives it."

In biblical times, a vote was cast using a stone, black for guilty and white for not guilty. Christ's sacrifice meant that the white stone had been cast for us.

Our house was in the little town of White Stone. Just as God provided daily sustenance each day for the Israelites in the Old Testament, He was giving it to us. Throughout the journey of Bob's cancer, God provided just what we needed each day, just when we needed it. God was so faithful. It was clear we should name our home *Hidden Manna.*

Bob mustered the strength to hang a hand-painted board with that name on our fence. I took a picture of him kneeling beside the white fence with our new sign, his arms around our faithful dog, Ginny, a big smile on his face.

God had provided this home for us before we knew Bob's cancer had spread. Now, it was a beautiful, hidden place of solace that we had not known we would need so much. Regrettably, throughout our 27 years of marriage, Bob and I were often too busy or preoccupied to savor such treasures. God had used cancer to slow us down. Later that day, Bob and I lay on the sofa, holding each other close. He knew he had only weeks or maybe months to live.

"Who can explain how love can grow in the midst of slow-motion devastation of the physical?" he asked. Then he answered his own question. "From an earthly perspective, it's totally illogical. It can only be evidence of the Divine."

God's love is inexplicable from human terms. How could love grow stronger as Bob's body weakened? From a human, "romantic" perspective, it makes no sense.

I had so often looked for the "big" things to demonstrate evidence of God, when in reality, God most often comes to us personally in whispers and quiet ways.

"Bob," I said to my husband, "this is so hard! I've never felt closer or more in love with you than I do right now . . . and I know it's all going to be taken away."

"True," Bob said. "But didn't the one require the other?"

CHAPTER 9

AN END, AND A NEW BEGINNING

"Joys are always on their way to us.
They are always traveling to us
through the darkness of the night.
There is never a night when they are not coming."
Amy Carmichael

Not too long after our last trip together to White Stone, hospice nurses arrived at our home in Richmond. I had been a hospice nurse, but never imagined my loved one would one day be on the receiving end of their gracious care. Hospice arranged for the delivery of a hospital bed. We set it up right next to the bed we had shared for more than 25 years.

45

One morning, I woke up and looked over to see Bob sitting on the edge of his hospital bed staring at his entwined fingers—pondering and examining them. Not sure if he was confused, a common symptom of liver failure, I asked him what he was doing. He looked up at me, his fingers still folded into one another, and said, "We truly have become one body, haven't we?"

God had done a miracle in our marriage.

Each night before bed during those sweet, final days, we would pray a prayer together:

> *O Thou who art from everlasting to everlasting,*
> *I would turn my thoughts to Thee as the hours of darkness and of sleep begin.*
> *O Sun of my soul, I rejoice to know that all night*
> *I shall be under the unsleeping eye of One who dwells in eternal light.*
> *To thy care, O Father, I would now commend my body and soul.*
> *All day Thou hast watched over me and Thy companionship has filled my heart with peace.*
> *Let me not go through any part of this night unaccompanied by Thee.*
> *Give me sound and refreshing sleep;*
> *Give me safety from all perils;*
> *Give me control of my thoughts, if I should lie awake;*
> *Give me wisdom to remember that the night was made for sleeping, and not for harboring of anxious or fretful or shameful thoughts.*
> *Give me grace, if as I lie abed I think at all, to think upon Thee.*[5]

There's no handy instruction book to tell you how to soften the blow for your children as their dad is dying. Bob gathered the boys together to let them know how proud he was of them: their characters first, their accomplishments second. He wanted them to know he was at peace, and to assure them he knew he was going to heaven.

On March 24, 2005, Bob woke up in time to celebrate with our son, Grant, who had just received an acceptance letter from the prestigious Wharton School of Business. I took a photo of the two of them sitting on the edge of the hospital bed, huge smiles on their faces, holding the acceptance letter between them. It was a good day.

That afternoon, though, Bob became increasingly weaker. He started talking about going on a trip; he needed to check reservations and pack his bag. Teasing, I told him that the only trip he'd be going on would be to heaven. Even then, I didn't realize he'd make his trip that very day.

Bob died peacefully in our bedroom that evening. It was Maundy Thursday.

Two days later, on Easter Sunday 2005, God gave me such a tangible sense of the resurrected body that we have in Jesus Christ. God has indeed swallowed up death in victory . . . but here on earth, we cannot see the reality of resurrection and eternal life. I asked God to help me cling to this awareness in the days and months ahead, to help me keep my eyes focused on the prize of heaven that awaits those who believe.

On Easter Monday, we laid Bob to rest in the spot we had chosen at Richmond's Hollywood Cemetery, inside a chapel-like mausoleum with stained glass windows. It sits on a high bluff overlooking the James River.

Oswald Chambers wrote,

> . . . *a river touches places of which its source knows*
> *nothing, and Jesus says if we have received of His full-*
> *ness, however small the visible measure of our lives, out*
> *of us will flow the rivers that will bless to the uttermost*
> *parts of the earth. We have nothing to do with the*
> *outflow—this is the work of God that ye believe . . .*[6]

Though faced with many obstacles during his last 5 years, Bob gave us all the gift of influencing our hearts for life in the way he approached his death. He was grateful for his blessings, courageous in facing cancer, assured of eternity with his God, and full of hope that his wife and sons would continue our lives in joy and peace.

I was so grateful. But the fact was, the man who had been my husband, lover, companion, life partner, and soul mate . . . was gone.

I did not know what to do next. Through my grief, anger, and tears, I prayed desperately to God, "Please, rebuild my life!"—because I knew I could not.

CHAPTER 10

IDENTITY CRISIS

"This is what life is about. It is being sent on a trip by a loving God, who is waiting at home for our return and is eager to watch the slides we took and hear about the friends we made. When we travel with the eyes and ears of the God who sent us, we will see wonderful sights, hear wonderful sounds, meet wonderful people . . . and be happy to return home."
Henri Nouwen

I knew that Bob was now home. No more pain, no more suffering. His sight was clearer than it had ever been. We sang "Be Thou My Vision" at his funeral; it was so perfect for this ophthalmologist surgeon. I prayed that God would give *me* vision for the days ahead.

Even though I'd had time to prepare for Bob's death, it was still hard to grasp the reality. I knew, because of our faith in Jesus, that I'd see him again. But for right now, he was gone. I would no longer hear his laughter, enjoy his quick wit, or feel his embrace.

Before his passing, I arranged for the original reel-to-reel audio tape of our 1977 wedding to be put onto a CD. We'd never listened to the recording in all of our years of marriage. Bob never had a chance to hear it; it arrived after he'd died. But it was probably more for me anyway.

I wept as I listened to it. Our young voices made it sound like we were about 15, repeating the vows we'd written. We promised to love each other for as long as we both would live, to console and comfort each other in times of confusion and sickness and adversity. We had honored those vows, some-times by the skin of our teeth, sometimes by sheer will, and sometimes out of obedience to God.

But I knew that ultimately, God had honored and richly blessed our commitment. The Bible talks about a couple be-coming one flesh, one body, and that was indeed the super-natural work that God had done in our marriage. So now our "one body" had been torn apart. I wondered how I'd go on when half of who I'd become was gone. It felt like a gap-ing wound, with no remedy to stop the bleeding, apart from family, friends, and faith.

As the weeks and months went by, it felt like everyone else got back into their usual schedules. Except me. My "new normal" was uncharted territory. My boys were back at col-lege or their jobs. I was 51 years old, a widow, at home.

Alone.

Even though I'd been involved in ministry outside the home, for years I had primarily defined myself as a wife and mother. As I reflected in the quiet hours by myself, I realized that I'd also defined myself by what other people thought of me . . . by what kind of neighborhood I lived in, where my sons went to school, and what my husband did for a living. I knew these things were superficial, but now I realized I had unconsciously bought into some of the cultural trappings— prosperity, position, and performance—of the American view of success.

Now I felt stripped. The roles I had inhabited for years had vanished. Who was I, really? I felt like the kind of person people look right past at a party, scanning the room for someone more interesting.

At the same time I was feeling this identity crisis, I also had to make some tough decisions. I was not left with a monetary safety net adequate for a single woman with a life expectancy of 40 or more years, and two sons yet to be launched. I needed to reduce expenses, so I made the hard decision to sell our home. It was far too big for my needs anyway. And I wanted and needed to find a meaningful job. The thought of putting together a résumé—after not having a paid job for decades—felt both ludicrous and frightening. I looked into reinstating my nursing license. I explored getting certified to sell real estate. I considered opening a small business. I thought about working at ICM.

In the challenge of figuring out what I would do next and how I would keep afloat, I knew all the right answers, intellectually. I knew that God would provide for me and my boys. I knew that all things ultimately work together for the good of those who love God, and that God was my Father, and I was His daughter.

People told me that God had great plans for me, that He would not give me more than I could bear, that all this would work for good. These things are all true, but they aren't buttons we push, as if God is a cosmic Coke machine, and happy results tumble right into our lives. I was impatient with pat answers. I was struggling, in a deep and fundamental way, with who I was and where God was really leading me. I had not much liked the plans He had served up in the form of Bob's disease, pain, death, and my own bereavement!

While I knew God's promises of comfort and assurance, I was also angry. I was angry that Bob had died. I was angry about my grief, loneliness, and insecurities about my future. I was also angry that my boys had lost their father.

I wrote in my journal,

Lord, I can look to the future and see either an empty black hole or an empty clean slate. Lord, I want you to write my future. Help me today to rest in the assurance that you are holding me in the palm of your hand and that I can trust you to bring good and bear fruit from my life. I pray that one day there might be joy again. Lord, please help me to know those things in my heart and soul.

A friend from Canada sent me these verses from Psalm 27:13–14, "I am still confident of this: I will see the goodness of the Lord in the land of the living. Wait for the Lord; be strong and take heart and wait for the Lord."

Little did she know how much I needed that reminder! Waiting was too hard for me. I was impatient and wanted to take control myself. I confessed to God that I could do nothing apart from Him, not even wait.

When I look at my journals from that hard season, I'm incredibly grateful. Grateful for the reality that God lovingly walks with us in our anger, grief, and pain. God knows what it feels like to be a human being. Jesus experienced earthly loss, tears, fatigue, anger, abandonment, and far more pain that I will ever know. He is well acquainted with our sufferings. He does not expect us to respond like cheery Christian robots when we encounter sorrow and loss.

My sister Cindy, the pastor, reminded me of the familiar words from the 23rd Psalm that I'd memorized as a dutiful little girl. The psalm promises that when we walk through the valley of death, we will not fear evil because the Lord is with us. Cindy reminded me that I couldn't walk around the grief and pain. I couldn't float over it. I had to walk *through* it. The Message says it like this: "Even when the way goes through Death Valley, I'm not afraid when you walk at my side. Your trusty shepherd's crook makes me feel secure."[7]

It's one thing to memorize Bible verses as a child. It's another to know, and depend on, their counterintuitive reality as an adult.

As was becoming my usual pattern, the scriptures came even more alive for me in a faraway place. Five months after Bob's death, I went with ICM to Tanzania.

PART 2

COOPERATING WITH GOD, IN *HIS* MINISTRY, AROUND THE WORLD

CHAPTER 11

GOAT CAKE AND THE HORNS OF A DILEMMA

"God breaks up the private life of His saints, and makes it a thoroughfare for the world on the one hand and for Himself on the other. . . If through a broken heart God can bring His purposes to pass in the world, then thank Him for breaking your heart."
Oswald Chambers

After a long set of flights, we arrived in East Africa. Our Tanzanian partners drove us along busy streets filled with people peddling on bicycles, walking, and packed and stacked into ancient vehicles. Colorful markets displayed strange, beautiful fruits and traditional goat cake.

Goat cake is not a cake. It's basically a cooked goat, its head still attached and its horns intact. I wasn't quite sure how I felt about that, but I chewed away, honoring the generous hospitality of our Tanzanian friends.

We visited beautiful white and blue churches in village after village. People spilled out of the buildings, dancing and leaping with the joy of the Lord. I breathed the clear African air and waved at the small children who would run to greet our minibus, happily shouting, *"Mzungu! Mzungu!"* *White person! White person!* I hugged the women in the churches. Many were widows like me, but had experienced more hardship than I had ever known.

I also met young women with babies swaddled on their backs. They'd been working all day over an open fire to prepare a meal for our group. I met a woman who had walked 6 miles, balancing an enormous jug of water on her head so she could mix cement to build her church.

The elderly village matriarch grabbed my hand and gently pulled me into her small, thatched hut. Her wrinkled face lit up as she pointed to the picture of Jesus hanging on her mud wall. The only furniture on the dirt floor was a low table and some bed rolls. She hugged me and motioned for me to sit down, to enjoy the rich hospitality of her humble home.

I wrote in my journal,

Lord, You've touched my heart in so many ways. What a delight to move beyond my life of loss in Richmond to see your hand at work in Tanzania! It's been so refreshing to see the fervor of the believers here, to be reminded how unimportant the things of the world truly are, so great to be reminded of your "Bigness,"

*to get a fresh picture of eternity, to feel the joy of using
my gifts for your Kingdom. Thank you that I have felt
the Holy Spirit at work in my soul, restoring my spirit.*

As our little bus jolted and bumped along a road near Morogoro, in the north of Tanzania, Dad and I sat together, taking
in all that we had seen and heard. He turned to me with a
serious look in his eyes.

"Janice, do you really want to reach the world for Christ?
Can you imagine any other stronger way to do it than helping
lead ICM? Are you ready to serve as chairman of our board?"

God was clarifying His call on my life. And while I was
overwhelmed at the thought of leading ICM, I was also struck
with the opportunity God was giving me to serve alongside
my father. God had given Bob and me 5 years to restore and
relish our relationship, and we took advantage of that time.
Why wouldn't I be just as intentional and build my relationship with my father?

Dad has always been a hard-driving man with high expectations of himself and everyone around him. He was of
the generation of men who avoided showing emotions or
affirming others readily. There was never any doubt about his
tremendous love for God and his passion to share the Word
with the world. God had used his creativity and availability
in extraordinary ways.

This would be an opportunity to learn from my dad and
to help lead the ministry into the next generation, establish-
ing it for a time when my dad would be gone. I'd served
on ICM's board of directors for years. I knew the ministry
well, and I knew it wasn't the Promised Land . . . but now
I distinctly believed that God was guiding me in the desert

aftermath of my husband's death, bringing me to a new, green place of service for Him.

I wrote in my prayer journal,

> *You must equip me, Father, for what You want me to do to further Your Kingdom—and it certainly seems that You've laid ICM in my lap. Please, Father, clarify my motives—my longing to serve You, please You, and do Your will, not to please my dad. But if ICM is where You want me, then that's where I'll be!*
>
> *Lord, I ask for Your wisdom, Your love, Your patience with Dad—guard our relationship—help him to respect me as a 52-year-old woman and not his little girl. Help me to respond to him as Your beloved daughter and not as a rebellious teenager!*
>
> *Help me to live in the light of Your love for me and Your will for my life as the benchmark!*

Even as I saw how God was strengthening my relationship with my father in Tanzania, it was also a sweet, sweet time with my mother. Maybe it was sleep deprivation, but we giggled together like little girls as we climbed into our twin beds at night in little hotels in the bush. Mom would tuck me in, smoothing worn sheets under the draped white mosquito netting that hung over the splintery bed frame, then she'd climb in, teasing me, "Oh, Janice, it's just like we're princesses in the royal palace!"

Soon after this trip, my mother's challenges with memory loss would become obvious. So these memories with my mother, now gone for her, remain precious and alive for me.

At other points on the trip, I saw my parents—at the age most people don't even think about getting up from their recliners—hugging our Tanzanian sisters and brothers, asking them questions about their lives and what they needed. We shared in heartfelt worship and laughed as we ate roast goat and sipped our bottled Coca-Cola.

Our last night in Africa, the team leader distributed small stones to each member of the team, meant to serve as reminders of our experience. Emblazoned on the stones were words like "hope," "trust," and "love."

The word on my stone was "rest." I held it in my hand, rubbing its smooth surface, thinking of the great verse from Matthew 11:28, in which Jesus says, "Come to Me, all you who are weary and burdened, and I will give you rest!"

During the years of Bob's cancer battle, I hadn't known much rest. In my widowhood, it didn't matter how much sleep I got, I hadn't had real respite. I would often wake in the middle of the night, unable to get my bearings, heart racing. I had felt anxious and overwhelmed by the many responsibilities and decisions I now had to shoulder alone.

Somehow, on that trip to Tanzania, God gave me a fresh sense of His presence and power. My African brothers and sisters nourished my soul. I felt a renewal of relationship and purpose with my dad. I had real rest under that frayed mosquito netting, laughing with my mom. And I felt a rekindling of trust and hope.

CHAPTER 12

AN UNEXPECTED JUNGLE CONFIRMATION

"You and I don't live in a series of big, dramatic moments. We don't careen from big decision to big decision. We all live in an endless series of little moments. The character of a life isn't set in 10 big moments. The character of a life is set in 10,000 little moments of everyday life. It's the themes of struggles that emerge from those little moments that reveal what's really going on in our hearts."

Paul Tripp

If I felt new hope in Tanzania, it was hard to maintain it when I returned home to Richmond, Virginia. I had to jump right into preparing our home for sale. I had to put stuff in storage and "stage" it so it would appeal to outsiders. I had to pack up family photographs and mementos that might turn off potential buyers. I had to dismantle Bob's office and give away medical books, research papers, and diplomas. I felt like a robot, automatically moving through each day's tasks, detaching myself emotionally so I wouldn't feel sad.

Thankfully, I got a contract on the house right away. But to me, this was more than a business transaction. It was the literal closing of the door to my former life, and moving not just boxes and furniture, but my whole self, to an unknown future.

I wrote in my journal, which was, by now, getting pretty ragged.

> *Lord, help me to trust in you for my future, whatever it is. Help me to be reassured! HELP!*
>
> *I know pride is involved as I've "shown off" my home to potential buyers. Lord, help me to lay aside the pride of this world. The lifestyle of a doctor's wife is gone now. I know I've been prideful about all of that—the house, the nice car, the jewelry, the accomplished husband. Lord, I pray that You please take the pride away—help me to find all my worth and joy in You alone.*
>
> *Help me to move forward and not dwell on the life that was. Holy Spirit, so fill me that I hold the things of this world with a loose grip. I don't want to lose hold of the memories and joys of my life, but please release me from the hold of possessions and trappings. Lord, help me look to You alone to define who I am and not possessions or title or position.*

I also struggled with sadness about disrupting our sons' memories. In selling their childhood home, was I reinforcing their father's death and further upsetting their security?

I realized that my sons were not always the most communicative people in the world, and they really weren't going to share their deepest feelings with me. That was okay; we were (and are) different. I couldn't fix all this loss for them. I wrote in my journal as I prayed, "Lord, help the boys as they must each deal with all the changes thrust upon them this year. Help us all to find our true home in You!"

It was December of that same year of flux, grief, and real estate headaches that I learned more about my true home by leaving my temporary home again. This time, I went with a group from ICM to Peru. (I should note that I was hobbling on this trip, having kicked our obstinate lawnmower because it would not start when I needed to blow leaves off the front yard. I missed Bob in many ways, both large and small, and having to maintain our yard was one chore I could have done without!)

Dad was on this trip as well, along with Ellen Vaughn and several board members and friends of the ministry. We flew into Lima, and then took a northern flight, eventually making our way along the Amazon River into indigenous Quechua areas where we've built many churches with our partner, Miguel Quicaña.

It was there that God solidified my decision to commit myself, unequivocally, to working full-time with ICM.

Miguel had endured more than I can imagine. He is from a big, close, godly family. His grandfather was a well-known pastor named Justiniano. His cousin Rómulo translated the entire Bible into one of the Peruvian Quechua languages.

Beginning around 1980, Peru was plagued by a Maoist guerilla insurgent movement called the Shining Path. Their goal was to upend the authorities in Peru and, through revolution, create a "pure" communist state. Toward that end, they threatened, murdered, and abused ordinary villagers.

In 1989, Miguel's grandfather, Justiniano, had welcomed visits from American missionaries. He was enthusiastic about partnerships between American and Peruvian Christians. This brought him to the attention of the guerillas. They were suspicious of his connection with the United States.

Justiniano pastored a church in Chakiqpampa, in a Quechua area in the north of Peru. Guerillas burned down his home and his church. He rebuilt them both, bigger and better than before. Young people continued to attend the church, in growing numbers. The revolutionaries were not pleased. A squad of masked rebels on horseback came to Justiniano's home. "Don't preach to the young people," they snarled at him, "or it's your life."

For the 83-year-old pastor, there was no choice. "I've got to be faithful to Jesus," he said. "I've got to preach His Word."

"Well," said the leader as he jerked his horse to leave, "you've been warned."

On December 10, 1989, the town got word that a group of guerillas were headed their way. Many of the people fled, but Justiniano and others stayed. "What could they want with me?" he said. "I'm just an old man." The next afternoon, eight hooded men arrived at Justiniano's home. They forced him to an open area where 200 insurgents waited. Convinced that the old pastor's hearing aid was a device for communicating with the military, a terrorist ripped it from his ear and crushed it on the ground.

As the remaining villagers watched and wept, the men beat and slashed Justiniano. They grabbed his white hair and forced his head back. Then they cut his tongue out, scalped him, and cut his still-beating heart out of his chest. Covered with blood, they shouted at the screaming neighbors, "If anyone buries this body, he'll suffer the same fate!"

They rode on to the next village, where they killed 45 more people.

Justiniano's widow mourned next to his body all night long. Meanwhile, her home was burned. Eventually, family members were able to bury what was left of their courageous grandfather. Miguel, then in seminary, came home from his studies. He wanted to comfort his mother and other relatives. They were devastated, but determined to keep on preaching the Gospel.

Two years after the murder, the entire extended family went to visit their grandfather's grave. On their way, they ran into a blockade set up by Shining Path guerillas. Dozens of cars and buses were trapped. There were more than 100 men shooting into the vehicles and robbing passengers.

The armed, hooded guerillas lined up the male members of Miguel's family. One of the terrorists approached Ruben, Miguel's young cousin, and shot him in the chest. Ruben whispered "Jesus!" as he fell, and then he was gone. Other guerillas sprayed machine-gun fire. Everyone fell to the ground.

Later, Miguel came back to consciousness. He lay very still, covered in his cousin's blood, so the terrorists would think he was dead, too.

After the guerillas left, Miguel pushed himself to his feet. Incredibly, he was still alive.

At the funeral for the relatives and friends who had died in the attack, Miguel's uncle spoke for the whole family—and for people all over Peru in those times of persecution:

> *Death is an ever-present reality for us. Humanly speaking, this is very painful, but we have to trust in the sovereignty of God. Our lives are in His hands and in His will. As for us, we will continue to minister in the conflict areas. Please continue to pray for us, because as you can see, there is a very high cost.*

Miguel Quicaña went on to become an engineer, agronomist, bank president, and Peruvian senator. He served on committees working with housing for the poor. He traveled to the U.S. in the mid-1990s to attend the National Prayer Breakfast in Washington, D.C., where he heard about International Cooperating Ministries. Miguel eventually left the Senate, founded an indigenous ministry, and became an ICM partner. He has coordinated the building of churches all over Peru. He felt that while his political career had been a good thing, now he was involved in a great thing.

He says, "I wake up every day today and I can see that my dream has come true. I have built beautiful churches for many congregations and pastors like my grandfather, who preach the Gospel in those places where poverty abounds, where people take advantage of the poor, enlisting them in violent causes, teaching them doctrines that only bring death and destruction. We teach them that Jesus brings peace and salvation. Young people who are involved in gangs, fornication, alcohol, drugs, and hopelessness find in our churches new hope and new life."

In 2006, Miguel took our small group on a trip deep into the jungle in northern Peru. Before we got very far, we stopped at a gas station to pick up a group of men who hopped into the back of a pickup truck that followed us. They all had guns. Old, rusty guns. We slowly realized that we were going to take the same road where Miguel's family members had been ambushed and killed, and our protectors were church members who had volunteered to protect us.

As our crowded vehicle bumped along the narrow way, I looked at the green jungle beside me. There were exotic parrots, monkeys, banana trees, and beautiful plants everywhere. Dad was next to me. On his lap was a fat leather briefcase that screamed to anyone who might see it, "I am full of American money!"

Of course, it was money for Quechua believers, but I didn't think any random thieves or terrorists on the road would care much about its intended recipients. Meanwhile, Ellen was sitting next to my dad, her eyebrows up, dutifully scribbling notes about our journey in her notebook as she scanned the jungle for bad guys with big guns.

We eventually arrived at our "hotel," deep in the Quechua jungle. The spindly rooms sat on stilts above a sewage pit. Pigs snorted nearby. Every room was subject to a perennial, slow rain of sawdust, as termites had their way with the wooden roof. There was torn mosquito netting—and occasional running water—for almost all of us. The beds were rickety, with poor, thin mattresses that were rich in bedbugs.

During the night, our new friends with the guns patrolled the area, protecting us from any threats that might emerge from the bush.

The next morning, someone did come from the jungle.

She was a platinum blonde, almost 6 feet tall, a striking Scandinavian who just did not look like she should be part of this environment.

We were drinking coffee outside on a rickety deck. She strode up to us wearing a draped scarf and holding a big toddler by the hand. We invited her to sit down. She told us, in beautiful, accented English, how she had met and married a Peruvian man while in college, and now she lived in the jungle and manufactured organic honey. Did we want to buy some?

At this point, she brought out several small jars of honey from her sack. Then she shrugged off her entire scarf and shirt and proceeded to breast-feed her child. Her large, *toddler* child. This was not something that ICM male board and staff members see every day. They did not know where to look.

My dad did not miss a beat. Keeping his eyes on her face, he continued to ask Miss Scandinavia kind questions about her life. In the end, we bought every jar of honey in her mobile inventory, with the hope she would just put her shirt back on and return to the jungle.

She did.

We left a little bit later, in a long Indian canoe, on one of the great tributaries of the Amazon. When we arrived at our destination, a church dedication service, the people were waiting for us with big hugs and smiles.

Our canoe glided to the riverbank. We trudged through mud to the church. Children cheered. The people there splashed pineapple juice over the doorways of their new church, a symbol of their love and welcome. Together, we all dedicated the church to the expansion of the Gospel in that part of Peru.

Our hosts had slaughtered a bull; it had been roasting for hours. There were huge pots of steaming rice and mounds of mangoes, papayas, and pineapples, picked that morning. Children played. Dogs and random pigs came and went. Solemn grandmas wearing bowler hats held babies on their laps. They welcomed us in as part of their family, hugging us close as if they'd known us for decades.

I realized that sometimes North American culture is so standoffish; we stand back, rather than draw near. I saw also that our friends in Peru had a different sense of time. They had anticipated our visit for weeks and would relish its memory for years. Our feast together was slow, sweet, and rich, the opposite of our often-overscheduled lifestyle at home.

As we left that beautiful community to head to the airport, my dad was sitting in the front of the vehicle. Those nice guys with the guns were still with us. Ellen and I were stuffed in the last seat in front of the storage area with all of the suitcases in the back.

"*Cheep! Cheep!*"

"I keep thinking I'm hearing a chicken," said my father.

Ellen and I looked at each other. We knew that our energetic and always-hungry interpreter, Elsa, had been given a chicken as a gift at our last stop. A poultry lover, she had put said chicken in with the luggage.

"Chicken?" we said. "How could there be a chicken?"

"*Cheep!*" responded the bird in the back.

"Well," my dad said, ever gracious, "maybe it's my imagination. But I could have sworn I heard a chicken."

Our consciences smote us.

"Dad/Dois," we said, "we are so sorry. It IS a chicken."

Peru is not like the United States. At the airport, Elsa checked her chicken for our domestic flight to Lima. Rolling along on the baggage belt, the chicken wore a little tag like she was a small suitcase with feathers.

"Elsa," we said, "what are you going to do with that chicken?"

She looked at Ellen and me as if we were stupid, which is entirely possible. "What do you mean?" she asked. "I am going to take her home, of course, and eat her!"

Well, by the end of that crazy trip to Peru, chicken or no chicken, I knew God's direction for me.

I returned home to welcome my boys for their last Christmas in their childhood home. I had sold it, thank the Lord, but I didn't have to move out until after the holidays. I felt a certain freedom . . . no big parties to host, no sporting events I had to attend, no need to perform or entertain or overspend. This was new ground. I asked for God to give me wisdom about how to truly celebrate the birth of Jesus at the same time that I truly acknowledged the pain of Bob's absence.

I also wrote in my journal, right near the end of that life-changing year,

> *Thank you, Father, for safety on the ICM Peru trip. Thank you, Father, for clarifying my involvement with ICM. I feel it is Your timing. Equip me, Lord; keep me humble always. Let me not lean on my own understanding, but upon You alone!*

The year 2005 rolled over to 2006: the beginning of familiar, yet radically new, adventures.

CHAPTER 13

A FEW GOOD MEN

"The best teacher is not the one who knows most, but the one who is most capable of reducing knowledge to that simple compound of the obvious and wonderful."

H. L. Mencken

As I transitioned—to my sons' bemusement—from being a stay-at-home domestic mom to a full-time ministry executive, a few godly men helped guide my way.

The first, of course, was my father.

I had profited from his training during my growing-up years. Now, as I settled into the everyday work of ministry, Dad's influence became part of my strategic thinking in many different ways.

One thing he drilled into all of us was to *focus, focus, focus!* That might not sound original, but you'd be surprised by how many individuals, businesses, and nonprofit organizations lose their way by taking their eyes off the prize. Dad showed me how to evaluate every opportunity before us—and there were many—by ICM's core calling to nurture believers and help our partners establish growing churches around the world.

Dad constantly encouraged us to look for where God was working, and then join into *His* work. This core practice completely aligned with my studies of Henry Blackaby's wonderful book, *Experiencing God*, which had shaped my thinking years earlier.[8]

Dad also taught me to be nimble when it comes to technology. He certainly didn't come from a high-tech background, but he pressed us to use the most current high-tech tools to meet the needs of the people we served. He urged us to study global trends, to discern how the world was changing, and to adapt our methodology for the greatest impact.

Dad had played a seminal role in the first Lausanne Congress on World Evangelism in 1974, which created a consensus strategy for reaching the entire world for Christ. At that time, leaders like Billy Graham and John Stott heralded the need for Americans to see evangelism in a new way. Rather than sending people to other lands with the Gospel— the missionary model of the nineteenth and early twentieth centuries—we needed to equip indigenous believers to spread the Word. Today, that mind-set is even more crucial, given the world in which we live.

Dad also emphasized that any missions enterprise is entrusted with God's resources. We may know that intellectually, but Dad lived it with exhausting precision. He leveraged every dollar, every tool, and every partnership for maximum output for the Kingdom. He never duplicated efforts.

The second good man who influenced me in my new role was Tom Pratt. Tom had served on Prison Fellowship's board of directors for many years, along with Dad. At the time, Tom was enjoying a successful career at Herman Miller. Then the design and furniture giant offered Tom the position of CEO. After much prayer with his wife, Gloria, Tom turned down that lucrative offer. Instead, he answered God's call, and the pressing desire of the ever-persuasive Chuck Colson, to move on from his board service to become president of Prison Fellowship in 1989. Tom led that ministry for 14 years, to its strongest and most innovative season as a ministry.

After finishing his run at Prison Fellowship, Tom was ready to retire. He looked forward to returning with Gloria to a quiet life at their lake home in Michigan.

No such luck.

Dad had long admired Tom's business savvy, wisdom, and heart for Christ. As tough a salesman as Chuck Colson, Dad prayerfully pursued Tom for ICM. Tom and Gloria prayed, and next thing we knew, Tom made a 5-year commitment, in 2002, to serve as our president.

So as I was tiptoeing in the door of ICM, Tom was waiting. He took me under his wing. Tom had been a wrestling coach as a young man, and so it was appropriate that he coached me as I was wrestling with God about taking on a leadership role at the ministry.

Part of Tom's job was to prepare ICM for the time when Dad would need to transfer the reins of the ministry to a successor. Tom had tremendous experience in board development and organizational structure. He understood the need for clear directives and procedures for the ongoing strength of the ministry. While my father was strong in vision and entrepreneurship, Tom was strong in creating systems that would help maintain the ministry for generations to come.

Tom's thoughtful and reflective nature was the yin to my father's go-getter yang. I learned a lot as I quietly watched them struggle with making decisions as they came from opposing viewpoints. It was a class in conflict resolution, based in deep brotherly love and mutual respect . . . usually solved at the end of the workday over cups of hot tea and Holland cookies.

Tom loved to noodle, brainstorm, and ask unexpected questions. He taught me how to probe assumptions and provoke people to dream of bigger ideas. I also learned a lot from Tom's deep commitment to the Bible, and his relationship with his wife and soul mate, Gloria. They were a team. Gloria took the group of volunteers my mother had gathered to pray for the ministry and grew it into an organized movement. Today, there are hundreds of people, all over the world, who pray daily for ICM's specific needs. They are part of Gloria's spiritual legacy.

We knew that Tom was with us for just a few years, as he and Gloria would eventually return to Michigan for that long-awaited retirement. I dreaded the day of the Pratts' departure.

We hired a headhunter to help us find the next president for ICM. We interviewed several great candidates, but we hesitated. At the time, the U.S. was in the midst of a dramatic economic downturn. We had no idea how the poor economy would affect ICM's donations, or if we would need to downsize in the future. It didn't seem like the right time to bring in a new outside executive, so we didn't hire a president just then, and I agreed to take on the role of CEO and executive chair of the ministry. I was humbled and astonished at what God had done. I believed He would equip me for the work He'd called me to do. And I imagined my late husband, grinning in heaven.

Then I rolled up my sleeves—thinking of such role models as Mother Teresa, Lottie Moon, Amy Carmichael, and Rosie the Riveter—and got to work.

CHAPTER 14

AWESOME ADVENTURE AND A LIFE-CHANGING CHARGE

"The great word of Jesus to His disciples is abandon."
Oswald Chambers

My first endeavor as CEO took me on a whirlwind trip around the world. I'm not sure what we were thinking when we planned it, but that crazy excursion turned out to be an unforgettable experience of God's creativity and faithfulness.

Randy Rich, an ICM development officer, knew several of the executives at K-LOVE/Air1, a huge Christian radio network. He introduced the organization to ICM. For a number of years, K-LOVE graciously allowed us to broadcast on-air fundraisers, encouraging their listeners to give to ICM building projects. Then Randy proposed a "Round-the-World Awesome Adventure" with ICM and K-LOVE, along with one of their on-air personalities, JD Chandler. People could submit an essay to win a trip for themselves and a guest. The team would visit China, Tanzania, and India, in 12 days. We'd report back so listeners could "travel" with us. At the end of the trip, our guests would choose which country of the three they wanted to be the focus of a daylong fundraiser.

Most of the winners had never been out of the country before. Now, here they were, preparing to go from frigid China to sweltering Tanzania, and intense, fragrant, and overwhelming India. I'll never forget being in the airport in Dubai at 2 a.m., on our way to our next destination. It might as well have been 2 o'clock in the afternoon. Thousands of people in exotic clothing milled around shops and restaurants. There was a big, shiny Rolls-Royce for sale, right in the middle of the airport. I guess wealthy oil sheiks purchase such things so they have something to bring home for the kids, but we didn't buy it.

K-LOVE host JD Chandler is a self-described class clown with a deep bass radio voice. He faithfully supplied a riotous running commentary for the entire trip. I'll never forget his front-seat reporting as our packed, dented minivan careened through the crazy streets of Delhi. He was sure that we were going to crash into a random cow, motorbike, elephant, or a car already well battered by the city's notoriously aggressive traffic.

JD's commentary also included observations on the wildlife of the Ngorongoro Crater. This is a deep, volcanic crater, the largest unbroken caldera in the world. Its Maasai name means "Gift of Life," and it teems with wildlife: lions, zebras, wildebeest, elephants, and comical pink flamingos. We were astonished by the beauty of this ancient wonder . . . but, in spite of its riches, we were disappointed not to see any giraffes. We were told that giraffes' long necks make it difficult for them to scale the sides of the crater, so they are left out of the Ngorongoro party, so to speak.

As our van sputtered back to our hotel, the biggest giraffe I've ever seen suddenly bolted across the road. We almost hit him. Then he pivoted his big spotted flanks on his long, awkward legs, rolled his heavily lashed eyes, stuck out his black tongue, and escaped off into the bush. We laughed until we cried. How in the world did God even make up a creature as hilarious as a giraffe?

The next day, we made plans to visit ICM churches on the far western border of the country near Lake Tanganyika, the longest freshwater lake in the world. We could only get to our destination by traveling in a 14-seat plane we chartered from Missionary Aviation Fellowship.

Weeks earlier, each ICM traveler had gotten an e-mail from an unknown person in Africa, asking for our weight. Most of us had ignored the odd message, not caring to share that information with a stranger. Now, when our group of strapping Americans showed up at the airplane hangar in Morogoro, the pilot skeptically looked us over . . . especially my son, Matt, who, at 6 foot 4, didn't look like he'd even fit on the petite plane.

Apparently, this pilot had sent the random African e-mail we'd all ignored. He proceeded to mortify us all by going back in the hangar and pulling out a huge scale. Each of us had to hop on and have our weight called out in a loud voice and noted on the pilot's clipboard.

He raised his eyebrows. "Okay," he said, "we have, uh, too much weight here for the plane. It won't be able to take off. So, you guys will have to leave people behind, luggage behind, or fuel behind. Which will it be?"

Well, we chose the luggage. The pilot did a few more calculations in terms of our combined tonnage and the weight of the fuel, and told us how much luggage we could bring with us. Three pounds per person. For three days of travel. While we were absorbing this unwelcome news, the pilot distributed thin plastic bags, like the kind you get at the grocery store. He didn't even ask us, "Paper or plastic?"

It became a group bonding moment as we carefully packed our flimsy totes. Together, we decided who would carry the common toothpaste tube, the group Bible, camera, and deodorant. Thankfully, we did get to carry our very own personal toothbrush. Regarding clothing, it was obvious that we would only be able to take what we were wearing.

We climbed on the tiny plane. The pilot told us where to sit, so our weight would be distributed in a way that the plane, hopefully, would not roll and crash. It was a wonky takeoff. Then, as we successfully climbed through the African air, we all just looked around at each other. We couldn't really talk; the propellers were too loud. There was nothing to do but laugh. It was a typical ICM traveling moment.

I should mention that my pants, which I had liked pretty well before that trip, became a little too familiar over the next 3 days. Because we were in some pretty dusty places, they were soon filthy. The second night at our little hotel, I sent them out for laundering, a common service in Africa.

I was pretty nervous, wondering what in the world I would do if something went wrong and my pants were not returned the next morning.

Fortunately, I did get them back, and we headed out very early to begin our 2-hour drive to take a rope-pulled flatboat across a narrow river. Then we drove another hour and boarded an ancient wooden boat. We sputtered across open water on Lake Tanganyika and disembarked on an island dotted with mud huts with thatched roofs. Tiny fish dotted the red ground, drying in the hot sun. The odor was distinctive.

Dozens of people gathered around us, full of huge smiles and not a little curiosity. Many of them had never before seen a person with white skin. As we looked up a steep hill, my heart filled as I saw a beautiful, white church with blue trim at the very top. The people had lugged all their building supplies first, by boat, and then up the dirt path to the highest place around—so that all the surrounding villages could see their church, built to the glory of God.

Our hosts escorted us to white plastic chairs, and the service began. None of us spoke Swahili, but we enthusiastically entered into several hours of worship. Then the music stopped. There was an expectant hush. To our surprise, several men walked down the center aisle of the crowded sanctuary, pulling an unhappy goat.

Oh my, I thought. *If that poor goat is going to be our lunch, we are going to be here for a LONG time.*

But the goat was, in fact, a gift from the congregation, in appreciation for all ICM had done to make their beautiful church a reality. We were overwhelmed by their sacrificial generosity. We felt like we couldn't receive such a fine gift, but we knew we couldn't offend them by denying their kindness.

So when we finally embarked in our less-than-seaworthy vessel to return to the mainland, Mr. Goat was in our boat. He kept making odd, anxious noises, particularly since nine of the church members were also crowded in with us, hitching a ride. Waves kept smacking against us broadside; overloaded, we were floating about an inch above the waterline. Matt and I exchanged looks with each other, knowing we might be swimming at any moment.

We finally made it to the mainland. Our trusty, rusty vehicle was waiting, and the church members kindly tied the poor goat to the top, up on the luggage rack. We made our way to a second church that was an hour or two away. There we worshipped with another congregation, and yes, they, too, gave us a goat in appreciation of our help.

So now we were toting two goats, lashed to the top of our vehicle. The rest of us, including our new best friends, the Tanzanian fishermen, were all packed inside so tightly that no one could move. We had to get back to the airstrip before dark, and so our driver sped crazily along the potholed roads. At every bump, the unfortunate goats would bleat in protest. PETA would not have been happy.

We finally made it to the airstrip. Since our weight had already been calibrated to the ounce, there was no way our unhappy goats could accompany us further. We thankfully gave them to our Tanzanian friends, hugged them farewell—the humans, not the goats—and sputtered off into the sky, back toward civilization.

A day or two later, on February 5, 2006, a third good man changed my life. We were visiting the large church of our partner, Dr. Barnabas Mtokombali. (When we first met Barnabas, he was a village pastor. As his denominational leaders saw his great gifts, he went on to pastor bigger churches over the years. Today, he is the archbishop of Tanzania Assemblies of God, responsible for thousands of congregations across his country.)

Pastor Barnabas called me to the front of the sanctuary. His church leaders fanned around me in a circle. Barnabas asked me to kneel. I was wearing a batik dress custom-made by my African sisters, and was clutching the Bible that Bob had given me years before. Its presence felt so appropriate as I made this transition to my new professional life without my husband.

There was a hum of expectancy in the packed sanctuary, and I could feel the electricity of the Holy Spirit as this circle of godly men and women commissioned me in ICM's work of the Gospel. Then Barnabas, living up to his biblical name as an encourager, proclaimed this charge to me:

> *To new Board Chair Janice Rosser Allen,*
> *I charge you with the following:*
>> *Be hopeful.*
>> *Believe that you can make a difference.*
>> *This responsibility is a challenge. Take it as an opportunity from God Almighty . . . He that began a good work in you will bring it to completion.*
>> *Fear not! For with God we can do everything.*
> *It is not by might, nor by power, but by my strength, says the Lord. May the Son of God empower you as you commune with Him . . . and He will empower you, the ordinary, to do the extraordinary.*
> *Five commendations:*
>> *Be a woman of integrity.*
>> *Be a woman with passion.*

Be a woman of the Word.
Be a woman who is Christ-centric.
Be a woman of prayer.

As Barnabas finished his charge, my face was wet with tears. Then I laughed as a dozen strong black arms reached down to pull me to my feet, and my African brothers and sisters congratulated me. I knew, by their faith and solidarity, that God had great plans ahead for us all.

It is wonderful to have such mountaintop experiences in the field. Back in the everyday life of the office, ministry can sometimes feel less exciting. Nevertheless, God's presence was real, even in the mundane moments of meetings, budgets, and strategic plans. I loved my work. I loved what God was doing through our little team in Hampton and our big team of partners around the world. I was blessed in a way I'd never dreamed.

Still, like any good endeavor, we did have our obstacles.

CHAPTER 15

WHAT'S SO GREAT ABOUT BUILDING CHURCHES?

"Our vision is to use any available method to share the Gospel, nurture believers, and advance the Kingdom, nation by nation. Just as Jesus told His disciples, He tells us today to 'Go and tell them who I am.' He has given ICM the tools to do just that. We are going into the world as He opens doors, using the vehicle of His Church and His Word to tell people who He is. I stand in complete amazement at the greatness of God and His power, which brings all this into being!"

Dois Rosser

One of the main issues I've dealt with over my years with ICM is that some people perceive us as simply a "church-building" ministry.

"What's the big deal about building churches?" they ask, perhaps thinking of U.S. communities that have a church on every street corner, many of which sit empty from Monday to Saturday. "The church isn't bricks and mortar; it's made of people. So what's the big deal about construction? What difference does a church building really make?"

Theologically, of course, we agree that the Church that Jesus Christ established 2,000 years ago is made of human beings, or "living stones," as the Apostle Peter put it.[9] The Church that Jesus said He would build—that the gates of hell would not prevail against—is not a nice edifice with a steeple or a cross on top. The Church is made up of redeemed people from every tribe and nation, people who will, one day, gather for eternity, proclaiming the wonders and glory of God.

Meanwhile, Christ-followers assemble in local gatherings, whether at The First Presbyterian Church of Hampton, Virginia, a small building on a mountain pass in Tibet, a jungle clearing in Colombia, or a small outpost in Algeria. The presence of these local churches changes their communities for generations. As Archbishop of Canterbury William Temple once said, the church is "the only organization that does not exist for itself, but for those who live outside of it."[10]

It would be wonderful if we could bring every person who has ever wondered why ICM gets excited about buildings to visit some of our churches overseas. These trips shatter U.S. stereotypes. There are few tree-lined streets with nice, underused churches in villages abroad. The developing world is not suburbia.

The people we exist to serve are, most often, desperately poor. They live in squalid dwellings in teeming urban centers, targeted by drug gangs and terrorists. They live in small villages far from civilization, tending crops. They live in freezing, remote places like Siberia or in shacks on stilts near the equator. They live in places where Christians are harassed and hated, and in jungles where animals are sacrificed to occult spirits.

The buildings ICM constructs for our partners are as varied as the cultures in which we work. Some do have white steeples and crosses on top. Some are two-story "community centers." Some are painted blue, or purple, or yellow. Others fly triangular banners that ripple in the breeze. Each congregation not only provides the land and the labor for these houses of worship, but also agrees to plant five daughter congregations within 3 years after construction is finished. They contribute a tithe of their meager offerings into a local "covenant fund" to help build another church for a deserving congregation. In this way, congregations first take ownership and responsibility for building their mother church; then they assume evangelism, discipleship, and financial accountability for five daughter church plants in the surrounding region.

In many parts of the world where Hindu temples or Muslim mosques dominate the landscape, church buildings offer tangible evidence that the God whom believers serve is real, that He is powerful, and that He cares. They provide a spiritual home for believers, a place to come together in fellowship, a school for growth and discipleship, and a safe place where outsiders can be included.

One such outsider was a Latin American woman named Maria.

Maria's heart stopped. She could not believe what the police had found. It just could not be true that her daughter was dead.

Maria was 30 years old. She lived in Mejicanos, a part of San Salvador, El Salvador's violent capital city. Two competing gangs controlled most of the area. One was the infamous MS-13, founded in Los Angeles by Salvadorans and brought back into their home country. The other was Calle 18. There were an estimated 25,000 gang members in El Salvador, responsible for some of the highest murder rates in Latin America, triple the homicide rate in Mexico.

The heavily tattooed thugs routinely extorted people, gathering protection money with guns and machetes stuck in their belts. They killed anyone they pleased. Life was cheap in the poor parts of El Salvador.

When Ellen and I met Maria, there wasn't anything distinctive about her appearance. She was one of many wonderful faces in a Salvadoran congregation. But when she sat down to tell us her story, her tears flowing, our hearts broke with love for our new sister.

Maria's experience is typical of poor Latin American women: a cycle of hopelessness passed down from generation to generation. Her mother worked as a janitor in the public toilets. Maria was put to work at age 7, selling tortillas in the market. She never went to school. When she was 12, a man made advances. At age 13, she gave birth to a baby daughter. The man left. Maria could not read or write. There were no jobs. She had no way to feed her growing girl.

At 15, Maria turned to her only alternative: prostitution. Her pimp got her hooked on drugs and alcohol. Crack and whiskey dulled her fear and shame.

Another man came, and at age 16, Maria gave birth to a son. She lived with the man and his mother, but had to keep selling herself. Sometimes she would wake up in strange beds and have no memory of how she got there. She was abused, betrayed, and disdained. She drank and drugged herself into a daily stupor. Life was too painful otherwise.

During the day, Maria sold socks on the street, or she went to the local garbage dump. She'd sit in the towering piles of trash, sifting through plastic bottles, used diapers, rotting food, and shattered glass, finding material she could recycle for the equivalent of a few pennies a day. At night, she would go to a run-down "nightclub," where her man would sell her to others. She would hide as much money as she could in order to feed her children and pay the "protection" money that local gang members required.

Maria stayed alive in this hellish existence for more than a decade. Her heart felt like a stone.

One night in 2001, she met a kind woman who gave her a plate of food. "I have a little restaurant," she told Maria. "Would you want to do some work for me?" Maria started cooking at the woman's café, grateful for this new friendship. When the woman invited Maria to her church, Maria didn't have much interest. Long before, she had decided God didn't exist or that He was too weak to save her from her misery.

But she respected her new friend, and so she went to church with her. Maria liked the music. She felt safe, and a tiny bit of something almost like happiness, when she came to the services.

On September 15, 2001, Maria made the decision to give her life, whatever there was of it, to Jesus Christ. Eight days later, she was baptized. A few days later, she felt something pulling her. Her old lifestyle was awful, but it was familiar. Something whispered in her head, "Go back to the bar. This spiritual stuff isn't natural. A drink or two won't hurt you."

Maria went back to the club. It was dark, full of smoke and predatory men, but the bottles on the bar were calling her name. She had a drink. Then she heard something different. "It was the Holy Spirit," she says today. "I knew I was new inside. The alcohol just didn't taste the same. I thought to myself, '*What am I doing?*'"

She got up. "Maria," a friend slurred, "stay with us!"

"I can't," said Maria. "There's nothing for me here." She left the bar, and from that point on, left her old life, grew in her faith, and embraced her new church family. She felt free. She loved serving the Lord.

About 5 years later, Maria's daughter, Ibania Maricela, was 17 years old. She was working in a different part of the city, a part of town controlled by a rival gang. It was common knowledge that people were not supposed to cross the city's invisible gang barrier. But Ibania could find no other work.

One day she didn't come home. Maria became increasingly worried. She and her friends from church searched frantically for Ibania. They called the police. They prayed. Time went by, and then Maria got the call that stopped her heart. Her daughter had been found. The police officer on the phone asked Maria to come to the city center to identify her body.

Maria caught a bus and went to the location.

Yes. It was Ibania, and the gang had made her into a warning for others. Her head was on the sidewalk. Her torso was in the gutter. Her arms and legs were in a pile in the city square. Maria identified her to the police, half-heard their brusque report, and got back on the bus. She was weeping and shaking, unable to comprehend this nightmare.

"O, God!" she moaned. "I cannot do this! I am too weak to survive this!" The oblivion of a whiskey bottle or a crack pipe seemed like the only options for relief from her excruciating pain. Then, in her heart, she heard a phrase from a Bible verse she had memorized. God had said to the Apostle Paul, "My grace is sufficient for you, for my power is made perfect in weakness."[11]

"When I am weak," Maria thought, "*God* is strong. He will not let go of me. He is with me. I can't survive this without Him: He is stronger than all this pain and evil. *Él es más fuerte.*" He is stronger.

Maria did survive that terrible day in 2006, and all the days that followed. Today, this is how she describes it: "I give the Lord the glory and the honor *because He has not let me go!*"

Maria's family members are now all believers. She serves as the director of evangelism and the director of hospital ministry for her ICM church. Maria knows firsthand the power of evangelism, and her own suffering has made her an empathetic and compassionate comforter of those in pain. Thanks to some friends of ICM, who got her started with a grill, a refrigerator, a cart, and food supplies, she now has a thriving little *pupusa* business. *Pupusas*—the traditional Salvadoran dish made of thick, handmade corn tortillas filled with cheese, meat, or beans—have allowed Maria to support herself.

Her son is active in her church as well. He and his wife have a spunky little toddler girl who is the joy of her grandmother's now-tender heart. The little girl's name? *Ibania Maricela*, in honor of Maria's beautiful daughter who was killed so many years ago.

We were in Guatemala recently, next door to El Salvador. When Maria heard about our impending trip, she made plans to come from El Salvador at her own expense. "I have been helped so much by ICM," she said. "I want to give back. Let me cook for you!" So as our little bus went to churches and children's care centers all over the cities and countryside, Maria, her pastor, and several helpers traveled with us. Maria hauled water and supplies and cooked over outdoor fires to make our meals . . . the best *pupusas* you'd ever want to put in your mouth!

Maria is in her early forties now. It is God's miracle that she is alive and well, and brimming with a powerful sense of joy, love, and peace. She has been delivered from the hope-lessness and abuse that permanently trap so many women in this part of the world.

International Justice Mission (IJM) identifies Guate-mala as "the most dangerous place for women in all of Latin America." Sexual predators go unrestrained, with only 6 per-cent of reported cases of sexual violence eventually reaching a verdict.[12] (Imagine the number of unreported cases.) When predators know that their assaults are unlikely to face any consequence, sexual violence becomes a relentless, everyday threat for children.

Because of this fact, and other needs, our ministry is increasingly building church-based children's Hope Centers. Church volunteers welcome children from the neighbor-hood. They feed the kids a healthy breakfast, a nourishing lunch, and provide snacks during the day. They teach read-ing, writing, and basic hygiene. They instruct the children in biblical principles and Jesus' teaching. They give out lots of hugs, comfort, understanding, and love.

One such church and Hope Center in a tough area is called Galillea. The church has about 200 members. The pastor,

Violeta, is a powerhouse. Her congregation serves about 150 children every day. They are a lighthouse in their community of about 6,000 people.

Two sisters from the area went through a tragically typical trauma. Their biological father had left them long ago. Their mother worked at a menial, demanding job, scraping together a living. While she was gone all day, the girls—ages about 8 and 10—would go to the cornfields to work. They'd each earn the equivalent of a quarter each day. And every day, four or five of the men who also worked in the fields would rape them. Their supervisors turned a blind eye.

Pastor Violeta found out about the abuse. Church members went to the children and told them about the Hope Center. "We want to come," the older girl said, "but we need the money we are making, so we can help our mom." The church members wept. "We will pay you each a quarter a day to come to church," they said. "We want you to be safe from harm!"

Today, it's no surprise that these girls are dealing with post-traumatic stress, but they are learning to trust, to sing, and to feel love—from the church people who they can see, and from Jesus, who they can't see. Their teacher walks them home every day, so she can protect them. The girls are gradually learning to feel secure. For them—and so many others—the church is truly a sanctuary.

When I visit churches like Violeta's, I always see a vision that is central to ICM: the truth that the Gospel, shared in purity and with love through a local congregation, is culture-changing.

Some friends put that vision to work in poignant ways.

Floridians Stephen Nobles and his wife, Aliceanne, had two remarkable biological children, Lindsay and Preston.

They also had a love for Guatemala . . . and about 9 years ago, they traveled there to adopt an at-risk 1-year-old girl.

Today, that girl is an animated, talented, and enthusiastic preteen named Anna. She is meticulously organized and keeps the rest of the family on track. Grateful to God and Anna's birthmother for such a wonderful gift, the Nobles wanted to give back.

Through ICM, they built two churches in Anna's home region of Guatemala. "We want to do everything we can," Stephen says, "to make sure that her birthmother hears the Good News of the Gospel. Because of Pastors Carlos, Gernando, and Miguel (the pastors who serve in that indigenous area), we pray that Anna's birthmother will come to faith in Jesus. We can't thank her enough for what she's given us. We want to give back to her, and to her wonderful country."

Pastors like Carlos and the others serve their flocks at great personal sacrifice. They've been offered more lucrative positions than working in churches in poor areas, but they are very clear about their calling. As one pastor said, "I didn't go to [a church] where the money was. I went where the *need* was. And by God's Spirit, what starts out as impossible ends up invincible!"

Sometimes church growth seems impossible because of dark forces. Today, in Guatemala, 72 percent of the population is under the age of 30, and there is a movement of young people returning to an indigenous Mayan spirituality.

Take, for example, Juan's story. It is a blend of ancient idolatry and modern temptations.

Juan grew up in a village where families typically have 12 or 13 kids. His dad had left his family. His mom beat him. He turned to alcohol for relief. He stole all the money his mom saved for food in order to buy liquor. He stole from others in order to buy drugs. He terrorized younger kids. He worshipped idols and sacrificed black chickens every Friday the thirteenth. The idols and the blood sacrifices didn't assuage his pain. He told his mom he could never go to church: God knew everything he'd done, and Juan felt like he was bound for hell.

One night, the police arrested him, tore off his clothes, and strip-searched him. They found his drugs in a body cavity and left him in the dirt.

Some people from the local ICM church found him. They helped him and invited him to church. He crept in, desperate for help. After the pastor preached about the power of Jesus, something very strange happened inside of Juan. "All the sudden, I was crying," he says. "A sister talked with me. She encouraged me to go the front after the service. I talked with the pastor. I received Christ!"

Years later, we visited his church and Juan shared his story. Then he asked an older lady to come forward. She walked to the front of the sanctuary, smiling, and Juan put his arm around her. "This is my mom," he explained. "For years, all I did was cause her pain. Now we truly love each other. Because of Jesus."

Do local churches in the hills and slums of Central America make a difference in individual lives, and in the community at large?

We have seen that they do.

CHAPTER 16

LOVE IN ACTION

*"A little thing is a little thing, but faithfulness
in little things is a great thing."*
Hudson Taylor

Earlier, I mentioned a few good men who have helped me along the way. There's another one who has helped to guide my path.

Back when my husband was alive, one of his closest friends was a wonderful guy named Geof Stiff. Geof and his wife Carolyn lived near Bob and me, and we were part of the same church. Our sons were buddies. Carolyn would be part of the faithful "band of sisters" that loved and prayed me through Bob's cancer and my early years of widowhood.

Geof had gotten his MBA at MIT, and then joined General Electric. He became then-chairman Jack Welch's personal financial analyst, then head financial planner for

GE, and a senior vice president for several of its insurance companies.

Years ago, around 1998, Bob and I invited Geof and Carolyn for an evening out with my parents. At the time, Geof had just returned from a church trip to the Dominican Republic. He was cranked up about missions and praying about leaving his corporate career to go into full-time Christian work.

Geof remembers Dad telling him that God doesn't waste any experiences in our professional lives, and that he didn't have to leave GE to serve Him. "Be patient and wait on the Lord," Dad told him. Another friend told him, "God has given you a strong Christian helpmate in your wife. Listen to her counsel!" Carolyn had encouraged Geof to wait until their sons finished college. Geof spent a profitable decade with GE, and then as senior vice president at Genworth Financial Retirement and Protection. He saw how God used him in relationships, stewardship, and witnessing within the corporate setting. He also served on ICM's board, chairing our finance committee.

Geof was also by my husband's side every step of the way through his cancer treatment and decline. Geof had known and loved Bob when he was a driven, busy, successful surgeon, but as cancer slowed Bob down, they truly became brothers in Christ. "He was an amazing man," Geof says today. "It was a transition for him to become very concerned about relationships; our friendship grew incredibly during the 5-year period of his cancer."

About 5 years after Bob's death, Geof was offered a generous early retirement package. His youngest son had just graduated from college. Geof and Carolyn believed it was now God's timing for them to enter full-time Christian service.

I encouraged Geof to consider ICM. And in January 2011, Geof became the ministry's president, and working with him has been one of the best blessings of the years since. His expertise in finance, systems, and strategic planning complement my own areas of strength, and I know Bob would be proud of us as a leadership team!

Geof recently took his family to dedicate an ICM church they had funded in Thailand. The church was for a big congregation of Lisu people, a tribal minority group with a long history in Asia. Their ancestors first came to know about Jesus through an indomitable missionary named James Fraser.

In the beginning of the twentieth century, Fraser was a 20-year-old British engineering student with a promising, conventional future ahead, but he couldn't stop thinking about Jesus' command to spread the Good News. He didn't want to be ashamed for not doing his utmost to fulfill Christ's Great Commission, so he joined the China Inland Mission, which sent him to a neglected, rural area of southwestern China.

In a muddy marketplace, Fraser noticed men and women of a particular tribal group who did not speak Chinese, wore their own distinctive native dress, and had never heard of Jesus Christ. He learned that these Lisu people were farmers, hunters, and animists who worshipped rocks and trees and offered animal sacrifices to ghosts. Fraser's heart broke for them. He would spend the rest of his life—until his untimely death from cerebral malaria in 1938—serving, evangelizing, and discipling his Lisu friends. He would also devise a written script for the oral Lisu language and translate the New Testament into it.

However, Fraser's first few years of ministry were full of disappointments. He was thrilled when the first Lisu family told him they had come to faith in Jesus, and then wept when they returned to spirit worship.

Fraser prayed earnestly. A less determined man would have given up and moved on. Then, about 6 years after he arrived in China, there was a breakthrough. Within about a 4-month period, 600 Lisu, representing 129 families, left the old ways and decided to follow Jesus. Fraser helped them start an indigenous church-planting movement, and many more Lisu in other villages also accepted Christ. The tide turned; missionary biographers say that the widespread conversion of the Lisu is one of the greatest stories in modern missions history.

Today, the Lisu people are recognized as an ethnic minority in modern-day China, and their religion—no longer animist, but Christian—is officially protected by China's communist government.

The Lisu are not only in China. They also live in Myanmar (formerly Burma), India, and Thailand. In Thailand, our ICM partner, Lu Chee Shi, is a descendant of one of James Fraser's first Lisu leaders.

When Geof, his family, and the rest of the team arrived at their new church, Lu Chee and 800 church members cheered in welcome. The church, called Rin Loung, is a mother church for others in the surrounding communities and overflows with five services a week. The members, who grow corn and nuts for their livelihood, give generously to the work of the church. And they don't just enjoy their fellowship and meet their own needs. They are constantly thinking about how to reach out, to bring others to the joy of the Good News.

While Geof was visiting, Rin Loung Church held an outreach medical clinic for Lisu people in the surrounding villages. Their new building includes a fellowship hall and a kitchen area. The enterprising church leaders had gotten a medical team of doctors, nurses, and dentists to come and work there for the weekend. They advertised the free medical and dental clinic by word of mouth in this area where there are no medical facilities.

Hundreds of people flooded into Rin Loung Church. Some had walked since the middle of the night to get there. Others had piled onto motorbikes and arrived honking their horns. Some were old, like the 104-year-old lady who smiled toothlessly at everyone. Others were sickly babies, just getting started in life. All were hungry for both physical and spiritual help.

The women of the church cooked huge vats of rice with red chili and chicken. The aroma of the savory food wafted through the church property.

In the end, 2,600 Lisu people visited Rin Loung Church during the 2-day outreach. As would be expected, there were long lines for medical services. Church members welcomed the patients. They asked questions about the visitors' lives. They brought them bowls of steaming food. They told them about Christ.

By the end of the weekend, 356 of those visitors had made a commitment to follow Jesus. "These nonbelievers had been watching Christians," our Lisu partner told us. "They needed to know that faith in Jesus changes lives. They needed to see love in action. When they did, they believed. We followed up with them; they were baptized and now are studying the Word of God."

The Rin Loung congregation has planted five daughter churches, with more to come. "God is truly working among the Lisu people through your partnership," one of the church leaders told Geof. "Through ICM church-building projects, we have seen so much good. The building projects really *do* change things for God's Kingdom!"

CHAPTER 17

WHOLE WORD, WHOLE WORLD

"The Word does the work.
The Word has power.
Devour this Word like your life depends on it.
Because it does."

David Platt

Ellen and I were in eastern India, with our partner Augustine Mathur and a group of ICM friends. We had just finished dedicating a church. Afterward, we all flowed out to a grassy lot behind the building. The sounds of children laughing, dogs barking, and drumbeats filled the air. As the sun sank below the horizon and a bright moon rose, the Indian women started to dance. They laughed as they tried to teach us their native steps and laughed even more when we tried to teach them the only dance we could think of at the time, the Hokey Pokey.

As we headed back to our minibus, we stopped by a small structure on the church property. It was more like a cave than a building. There was no electricity, and it was narrow and dark.

A dozen young women were crammed into that cave. They all had their Bibles, small flashlights, and print copies of a Mini Bible College handout in their Telegu language. Though it was late, and many had to go to school or out into the fields the next day, they were studying the Word of God.

Multiply that simple scene by about 170,000 Bible study classes over the years, and you begin to get a feel for the immense potential of ICM's Mini Bible College. It is the central means by which our congregations around the world disciple their people and reach out to draw others into their fellowships.

Our partner Augustine says, "Mini Bible College turns listeners into worshippers." He's right. MBC is a devotional overview of the Old and New Testament, a study of the Sermon on the Mount, and a biblical study of marriage and family. Its audio form presents 215 30-minute lessons. It is simple enough that any person, regardless of his or her familiarity with the Bible, can learn its core truths. It is deep enough to stimulate pastors who are trained in ICM facilities around the world. If digested, it stimulates people to a deeper understanding of God's wonders.

We would never have had this great resource if my dad had not studied under Dick Woodward's powerful teaching in the late 1970s.

Dick didn't look like much of a powerhouse. He called himself an "innocent little brown-eyed pastor" who struggled with such an inferiority complex as a youth that there was nothing complex about it—he was just plain inferior. After he discovered Christ and eventually became a preacher, he wasn't an eloquent orator in the usual style of big, booming, bass pastors of the day. He was a medium man with a low-key, conversational way of speaking. But he had an uncanny way of making the Bible accessible to people who couldn't access its truths on their own.

Dick was like the Apostle Philip in the New Testament story of Acts 8, when Philip connected with a government official who was riding in a limousine (of his day) and having a hard time understanding the prophet Isaiah.

> . . . the Spirit said to Philip, 'Go over and join this chariot.' So Philip ran to him and heard him reading Isaiah the prophet and asked, 'Do you understand what you are reading?' And he said, 'How can I, unless someone guides me?' And he invited Philip to come up and sit with him.[13]

You know the rest of the story. After Philip guided him through the scriptures, the man in the chariot came to faith in Jesus and asked to be baptized.

Similarly, Dick's Mini Bible College has been a guide for millions of people around the world to truly understand the scriptures.

When Dad served on Lausanne's International Congress on World Evangelization in the 1970s, he had heard how the Gospel had gone to places all over Africa in big crusades. The Word had been eagerly accepted. There were reportedly 16,000 people coming to Christ every day. But these new believers in Africa hadn't been further nurtured in solid studies of the scriptures. In the absence of real discipleship, new believers had been susceptible to false teachings, cults, and simply returning to their old ways.

This still happens today. As Pastor John Piper has put it, there's a prosperity gospel spreading abroad that sounds something like this: *Believe in Jesus, and your goats won't die, your wife won't miscarry, and you'll be rich!* This heresy, born in America, is strong on self and a false picture of God as a heavenly sugar daddy. It blows away with the first breeze of adversity.

Dad knew that believers had to put down deep roots in biblical truth. He believed that Dick's biblical teaching could be a powerful discipleship tool that could help new believers grow in maturity and equip them to nurture others.

Dick always said that my father "put legs" on Mini Bible College. For his part, Dad felt that you could have the best product in the world—the Word of God—but unless you distributed it, you'd be hiding your light under a bushel. He determined to distribute Dick's biblical teaching through every form available. Over the past 30 years, as technology has developed, that has meant radio, print, live-streaming on the Internet, in solar-powered audio players, and in SD cards that people can put in their cell phones. As we've said at ICM for years, if Coca-Cola can distribute Coke to every village around the world, we should be able to get the Gospel everywhere as well, using every means of technology possible!

The only downside to Mini Bible College is its name. Early on, when he was pressed by someone who needed to print a church bulletin right away, Dick titled his study quickly, without much thought. He didn't know that one day it would be translated into dozens of languages. Our partners in the field have told us that translations like "Small Bible University" or "Tiny Bible Class" or "Wee Holy Huddle" just don't cut it.

So we've encouraged our partners to name the study something that makes sense in their culture. In the former Soviet Union, Dick's study is called "Eternal Truths." In Spanish, it's "Bible Institute Air," and in Hindi and Bengali, we call it "Veda School." In Portuguese, it's "Encounter with the Word." And in Arabic, it's "In the Shade of the Word."

Similarly, our distribution of Mini Bible College has often followed opportunities we had no idea existed. We've just bumped into possibilities God has put in our path, and then used them. As Barbara Brown Taylor says,

> *Human beings may separate things into as many piles as we wish—separating spirit from flesh, sacred from secular, church from world. But we should not be surprised when God does not recognize the distinctions we make between the two. Earth is so thick with divine possibility that it is a wonder we can walk anywhere without cracking our shins on altars.*[14]

For example, ICM ran into a "divine possibility" through the current crisis in the Middle East. Though we can't describe much because of security issues, suffice it to say that we met pastors from closed and hostile countries through an unexpected opportunity. They connected us with creative ways to distribute our Bible teaching, and the Arabic version of MBC is now being used in refugee camps in the Middle East and Africa. Christians who have been displaced from their homes are learning its truths. Iraqi Yezidis and other ethnic and religious minorities, terrorized by ISIS, now have opportunities they did not have in their home villages.

One 14-year-old girl had fled from her home, alone. "In Syria," she said, "I had everything: a house, family, friends.

A normal life. But now I have nothing. Even my dreams are dead. I can't sleep; I hear the voices of my family. They were all killed in one night."

A pastor and his wife wept and prayed with this teenager. They shared the love of Christ, and she received Him. They also gave her an Arabic MBC audio player, so she could learn more about her new faith.

A Muslim refugee who similarly turned to Jesus said, "I lost everything in Syria. But I cannot lose Christ, because He is in my heart."

In a very different part of the world, God worked in a similar, timely way regarding the distribution of MBC. In Nepal, MBC teaching disseminates primarily through radio. We had one radio tower in Katmandu broadcasting Dick's teaching. Then, in April 2015, our Nepali partner asked if we could add more towers. He felt a strong leading from God to cover his entire country, not just the capital area, with the Gospel. After prayer, we gave the go-ahead for him to contract with 29 more radio towers.

One week later, on April 25, 2015, the nation of Nepal shook with an enormous, deadly earthquake. Eight thousand people died; more than 21,000 suffered injuries.

Only one of "our" 30 radio towers was damaged, and it was quickly repaired. So in the aftermath of that awful catastrophe, at their time of greatest need, people all over Nepal were hearing the Gospel message of hope as Dick Woodward's Bible teaching flooded the nation. Many came to new faith in Jesus.

Dick just could not have dreamed that his Bible survey would become a lifeline in places as disparate as Nepal and the Middle East!

After Dick finished writing the Mini Bible College in the mid-1980s, he didn't just rest in his accomplishment.

In spite of his quadriplegia, he maintained a fruitful ministry for the rest of his life. Cared for with tender expertise and love by his family, he did not allow his paralysis to immobilize his spirit. (Ironically, in light of the paralysis, he experienced chronic, debilitating pain, but he would not take narcotics. He wanted his mind to stay sharp.) He pushed hard every day, writing by means of his voice-activated computer, meeting with friends and the men he mentored, singing hymns at the top of his weakened lungs, praying passionately for everyone he knew, and generally expending himself for Jesus' sake. He always joked that his inability to walk or run meant that when he did reach the end of his earthly race, he would just roll across the finish line.

On March 8, 2014, Dick Woodward did cross his finish line. He didn't roll. Just after the moment of his death, I'm sure he leapt joyously right into the presence of God.

One of the heirs of Dick's legacy said it best. Frederick Mukendi, an ICM partner in Democratic Republic of the Congo, wrote this:

> *We have just learned about the departure of our Leader, Teacher, and Trainer, Reverend Dick Woodward, who we have come to know and love for some years now. His teaching has been and still will be the foundation and the guidance to our churches, correcting our marriages, shaping our doctrines, and illuminating our understanding through Mini Bible College. He is, and will always be, a blessing to our churches and pastors and mostly to myself and my family.*
>
> *What will be my excuse before God? What will be your excuse before God? If Dick Woodward could do what*

he did in the ability of his God, what will be your excuse with the same God? If Woodward could despise his pain and serve his God to the last day of his life and impact so many lives, even to my little village, what will be my excuse?

Let us continue to perpetuate the purposes he lived for. Our Pastor is not gone; he is still with us through his work, although he sleeps in death.

CHAPTER 18

IT'S SO COMPLEX

*"When the people of God get into the Word of God and
the Word of God gets into the people of God,
wonderful and miraculous things begin to happen."*
Dick Woodward

During my father's first trip to India in the mid-1980s, he
met a man named Emil Jebasingh and his wife, Ananthi. They had founded Vishwa Vani, an Indian-funded, indigenous outreach bringing the Gospel to places where it had
never been heard. In Emil, Dad found a fellow visionary and
a new partner. Though Emil died of cancer in 2013, Vishwa
Vani carries on boldly today, under the leadership of P. Selvaraj.
Its mission is bold: to reach 100,000 villages and 300 people
groups, developing healthy, reproducing congregations.

In 2008, we sensed God was positioning us to do something new. We brainstormed with Vishwa Vani to create a unique church-building model that would radically expand evangelism and discipleship. Indian church planters would travel into rural, unreached areas and survey villagers. They would determine local needs and see if there were any other Christian ministries present. If not, then the church planters would go to work talking with people about Jesus and starting a church as more and more men, women, and children came to faith in Him.

This is being replicated in village after village, and we're working with a new model to facilitate even more growth. We've been calling it a "Cluster Complex."

Each cluster—spanning a radius of 75 to 100 miles—consists of 25 mother churches, 100 daughter churches, four Learning Centers to equip local lay leaders, one Learning Resource Center to train indigenous pastors, and a child-care center for orphans. They all use the Mini Bible College curriculum in their own language. They have grown so quickly in one cluster that they have even built 125 granddaughter churches, all with local funds.

Needless to say, this is a big idea . . . and our 50-50 partnership with Vishwa Vani is a beautiful example of why we're called International *Cooperating* Ministries. There's no need for us to reinvent what Vishwa Vani is already doing so successfully, nor could we. We can give a lift and our own particular expertise to their ministry, but we don't need to put ICM's name on the beautiful complexes built through our partnership. All of us are interested in giving glory to God, not to our own ministry.

This cluster model is multiplying in tribal areas, and in one place so isolated that even the government had forgotten it existed.

Many years ago, Indian authorities dammed a large body of water in a rural part of eastern India. As a result, the native people in the affected area, called DK Parthi, were cut off from the rest of the world. They were hemmed in by mountains and water, accessible only by significant hiking or by boat. There were about 6,000 people, living in 38 different villages, on the newly formed peninsula.

An enterprising pastor had heard there were people beyond the mountain, and he hiked the rural paths to get to them. He found the people and shared the Gospel. Many responded. They learned the ways of Jesus, and gradually a band of believers was established in this isolated place. There were no roads, nor any other infrastructure. "The government had forgotten about us," said one village elder, "in spite of the agency in the big city that is supposed to take care of tribal people."

Dr. Nancy Croker, an ICM board member and passionate advocate for the ministry, visited DK Parthi in 2011. "It was so primitive, almost like we were visiting a tribe that had had no contact with the outside world," Nancy said. "They were so isolated and needy. But when we worshipped with them under a tent, we felt moved to let them know that God's people beyond their village had not forgotten them."

Two middle-aged sisters, as petite as 12-year-olds, shyly came up to Nancy, pointing at the cross she wore around her neck. Then they pointed to heaven. "I found out that these tiny women had 14 children between them," said Nancy. "And they were showing me that we were sisters in Christ, because of the cross."

Seeing the need, Nancy and others on the team wanted to build more than a church in DK Parthi. ICM's partner later submitted their building plan—which included not only a church, but also a medical clinic, school, and child-care center—to the villagers. They loved the proposal, but because of their poverty, it seemed impossible to the people that all this could actually happen.

Nancy, Ellen, and I, along with other ICM travelers, returned to DK Parthi in 2014, and we saw how the impossible had become a reality.

"As soon as we got out of the boat, I could feel a difference from my first trip there 3 years earlier," Nancy said. "Before, the people were wonderful, but they were so timid and downtrodden. Now they had a palpable exuberance."

Today, there is a permanent school for 300 students, a church, Hope Center, and medical clinic, and as is often the case in stories like this, once ICM established permanent, quality buildings in the area, the government finally "remembered" its forgotten people. In DK Parthi's case, that meant that government workers made their way to the village and dug a much-needed well. They put in roads. The people can now connect with the rest of the world.

The medical clinic serves about 30 people from outlying villages every week. Recently, they held an open house, and 260 people came, from 22 different communities. They suffered from everything from skin ailments to typhoid fever to malnutrition.

While we were there, one of the doctors brought a man and his son into the clinic. He had been outside the village and had seen the father running as best he could along the stony path on the mountain ridge, frantic yet determined to somehow get his son to a hospital about a dozen miles away. The dad didn't know that DK Parthi's clinic existed.

The little boy, 4 years old, was burning up with fever. Right on the road, the doctor did a simple test. He found that the boy was suffering from cerebral malaria, a killer in this area.

The doctor rushed the man and his boy to the clinic. He gave the boy quinine and other drugs, just in time. The child's life was saved.

"If we weren't here, so many people would die," the doctor said. "Because of this clinic, and this church, we are saving lives, both physically and spiritually, every day. It can be difficult here. Many people think of Jesus as one of many gods, since Hinduism has so many. They think of Him as foreign, or Western. But when we serve them—through this clinic, through our church, in the school, however we reach out to them—they see Him more clearly, right here in their village."

CHAPTER 19

DARK POWERS, BRIGHT CROSS

"How could I spend the best hours of my life working for myself and for the honor and pleasures of this world, while thousands and thousands of souls are perishing every day without having heard of the Lord Jesus Christ, going down to Christless and hopeless graves?"

C. T. Studd

The sun had just risen over the River Ganges. Burt Reed, Ellen, and I had hired a rickety wooden boat to take us out on the sacred river. We were in Varanasi, known as the holiest of the seven sacred cities in Hinduism. It is the spiritual capital of India and one of the oldest continuously inhabited cities in the world. Many Hindus believe that if they die in Varanasi, they are assured salvation, or *moksha*. Accordingly, many ill or elderly Hindus come to this city to die.

Most Hindus in this part of India are cremated. They believe that burning releases a person's spiritual essence from the physical body so it can be reborn, through reincarnation, into the next cycle of life. If the cremation is not conducted properly, the soul will remain unbodied. Restless, it will take to haunting relatives and neighbors.

The crematory fires in Varanasi burn 24 hours a day, 365 days a year. Families carry their loved ones to the muddy banks of the river. Priests wash the bodies in the water of the holy Ganges. They smear the remains with clarified butter, or *ghee*, which will help them burn. They wrap the bodies in white cloth, carefully tied and secured, then place them between thick pieces of wood. The amount of lumber depends on how much the family can pay. Bells ring. Priests chant. The dead burn. Watching, we felt like the scene was a physical representation of a spiritual reality.

It is considered a good omen if the skull explodes. Those remains that are not consumed by the flames are dumped in the sacred river . . . which flows with raw sewage, cow carcasses, and garbage.

In the morning mist we heard the tinkling of the bells, saw the endless fires of the crematoria burning, and waved to the visitors from around the world who had come to float candles and chrysanthemums on the river.

As we floated by the ghats—stepped areas that allow access to the water—we saw pilgrims stripping naked to purify themselves in the filthy water. Cows wandered up and down the steps. Their excrement was everywhere. Vendors peddled flowers and trinkets. Indian fakirs, or holy men, their faces smeared with white ash, posed for photographs. Lines of dirt-covered children, some with amputated limbs, begged for money on the stairs as their parents or owners lurked behind.

India is overwhelmingly Hindu, with a Muslim minority. Hinduism is not just a religion, but a culture. The current Indian government militantly proclaims that India *is* Hindu . . . and the Christians there are often targeted for violence by villagers who resent their presence.

Whether you are in the capital of Delhi, or in a village, sacred cows are everywhere. Tiny, beaten-up cars, donkey carts, bicycles, motorbikes, rickshaws, brave pedestrians . . . it's all a brightly colored party. Hindu temples are on most streets, where plastic gods and goddesses are set up to receive gifts of coconuts so travelers might have a safe trip down the undeniably frightening highways.

I've already mentioned one of our partners in India, an ebullient, animated brother named Augustine Mathur. Augustine, always smiling, fluent in multiple Indian languages, is a hospitable, fun, godly host. Based in Hyderabad, he's constantly on the move, assisting with baptisms in one area, dashing to help set up a church sewing center in another, traipsing through villages to share the Gospel, and encouraging pastors and workers everywhere. Spend time traveling with him, and you will come away exhausted, laughing, and invigorated, having witnessed many stories of God's transforming power.

In early 2014, Augustine gathered a group of about 30 pastors who had come to Varanasi for training and fellowship. Some had traveled 12 hours by bus or motorbike. Their stories were representative of the people they serve in various rural communities.

Almost all were from Hindu backgrounds; several had been Hindu priests. One is named Rakesh. As he told Ellen his story, he was full of smiles, busting out of a bright orange furry sweater vest that somehow survived the 1980s.

Rakesh grew up worshipping idols and inviting their power. As a young man, he started having terrible headaches, which got worse and worse until he could not function. He would roam in the jungle at night, looking for dead animals to eat. He gnawed on wood and ate whole bunches of green chili. His family frantically tried to stop him from eating his own stools when he would go to the outhouse. No one had the strength to restrain him from doing whatever bizarre action he chose.

Rakesh's family took him to Hindu and Muslim healers, to witch doctors, to anyone who could possibly help. People took their money, but there was no healing.

Finally, someone told the family about a church in another village. A friend and Rakesh's wife and his mother tied his arms and legs so he wouldn't hurt himself or others. They got him to the church. Then they loosened his bonds so he could walk in.

The church was full of people, and in the usual Indian custom, they had all left their shoes at the door so as not to dirty the floor. Rakesh picked up a shoe with his still-bound hands and started beating himself and howling.

The pastor, who was preaching at the front, did not miss a beat. "In the name of Jesus, SHUT UP!" he shouted. Then he went on with his sermon. Rakesh tumbled to the floor, silent.

After the service, the pastor approached his desperate visitors. "What can we do for you?" he asked. It seemed a rather mild question, given the situation.

The frantic wife spilled out the story.

The pastor, surrounded by elders, put his hand on Rakesh's head. Rakesh responded by screaming and struggling. "I rebuke you," said the pastor, "in the name of Jesus."

"I am not one; I am many," Rakesh's guttural voice responded.

"Are you five?" asked the pastor.

"We are more."

"Ten?"

"More."

"Twenty? Fifty? One hundred?"

Each time, the croaking, inhuman voice responded, "No. We are more."

The little pastor began praying in Jesus' name. By now, Rakesh was on the floor, spinning on his back. His eyes rolled and his joints convulsed, and then something came out of him. Rakesh's mouth foamed as he spat out a name, the name of the entity that had just emerged.

This happened over and over and over again. One of the elders had a notebook in hand; he took down each name.

For Rakesh, it was like electricity, or something stronger, jolting through his body. Tears poured down his face. His body jerked, over and over again. The pastor prayed, surrounded and echoed by the elders and the rest of the congregation. Time passed.

By the end of the night, Rakesh was weaker than a newborn baby. The ropes that had bound him, drenched in sweat, had been removed. The elder who had recorded each spirit's departure had 108 names on his list. The pastor prayed over him one last time, anointed him with oil, and gave him fresh water. It was the best thing Rakesh had ever tasted. A new, clean beginning.

Rakesh was baptized. He studied the scriptures under the care of his new pastor and elders. He went to an ICM Bible training center. And today, Rakesh is a pastor who visits 20 villages each week. He has established five churches and 78 Bible study groups, all of which use the Mini Bible College curriculum.

Drive about a thousand miles east of Varanasi and you will arrive in Tripura. This small Indian state is almost completely surrounded by Bangladesh. After World War II, when India came out from under British rule and was partitioned in 1947, large groups of Hindus left the area that is now Bangladesh (which was majority Muslim) and moved into Tripura. This state now has the only communist government in India, and a tribal movement there wants Tripura to secede from India. The largest tribal group is the Borok people, who speak a dialect called Kókborok.

In a little village several hours from Tripura's capital, many Borok people have come to know Christ.

One is a pastor named Naphurai. He works in places where local tribespeople worship spirits of trees and stones. Naphurai understands their practices, as he used to do the same.

"My grandfather was a demonic high priest," he says. "I learned much black magic. Since I was his first grandson, he wanted me to keep all of the traditions."

As an older teenager, Naphurai would take a shard of glass and pierce his own chest. He would catch the flow of blood in a large, supple banana leaf, and offer it to his god, a local deity named Gorai.

In spite of his blood sacrifices, he felt no peace. He was filled with anxiety and longings that couldn't be satisfied.

Naphurai met a missionary from New Zealand, who gave him a Bible in the Bengali language. Naphurai had read all of the Hindu scriptures and had no interest in the Bible. He put it aside. Then the missionary and another man visited his home, stirring his curiosity about Christianity. They told him that other people in the tribe were being baptized as Christians that day. Naphurai went with them to the pond to watch. Something in his heart cracked open, and when the missionary asked him if he wanted to believe in Jesus and be baptized, he surprised himself by saying, "Yes!"

"Under the water, my heart was changed," Naphurai told us. "I was a drinker, a fighter, always longed for alcohol and tobacco. But now, I felt so peaceful. I felt new and fresh, and my heart was light. No longings. I didn't know then what had happened; I came out of the water and saw everything as new."

Two people who were baptized with Naphurai that day were severely beaten by extremist neighbors and driven out of the village. Fearing the same for his son, Naphurai's father told him to hide in an abandoned house. Naphurai took his Bible with him, and in the long hours alone, started to read the New Testament. He said later,

I read about a child born to a poor Jewish family. I read the Sermon on the Mount. It changed me. As I turned page by page by page in the story of Jesus, I was so happy. I loved this man so much. And then the religious leaders hung Him on a cross! I felt so much pity and love for Him, and I was crying and crying. I had never heard about this God who hung on a cross.

As I was weeping, a bright light started coming into that room in that empty house. It was a shining, brilliant cross. I fell at the foot of the cross. I don't know how long I was there.

After some time, Naphurai got up. His soul was quiet. Eventually, he went to seminary. He became an ordained, church-planting pastor. Today, he works with ICM's partners in the northeastern villages of India, sharing the Good News of the God who hung on the cross.

CHAPTER 20

"IT IS BY THEIR BLOOD THAT WE KNOW JESUS."

"There are three stages in the work of God:
Impossible,
Difficult,
Done."

Hudson Taylor

One day in 1995, Burt was in India, meeting with some of ICM's partners. That same day, Dad had a visitor in his office in Virginia. He was a man with a vision for reaching Vietnam with the Gospel. Dad didn't miss a beat. He called his old friend and colleague. "Burt," he drawled into the phone, "since you're already in India, can you run by Vietnam on your way home? We need to get started in ministry there."

Well, Burt didn't miss a beat, either. He resourcefully went on to Vietnam and began to develop relationships there. Since then, ICM has built churches all over that beautiful country. And, as only God could design, some of our work there is woven into a story that God started back in the toughest days of the Vietnam War.

It was January 1968, and Vietnam rumbled with the thunder of war. It had begun quietly, years earlier, when a radical student called Ho Chi Minh first embraced Marxism. Now, Ho and his generals held North Vietnam. His guerillas terrorized the south, where South Vietnamese and American troops fought to stop communism's march on Indochina.

Bob and Marie Ziemer and their fellow Christian and Missionary Alliance missionaries were noncombatants. The tribespeople knew they weren't a threat and had relayed to the Viet Cong how these Americans had learned their language, how they ran a leprosarium, clinic, church, and school to help anyone they could, and how they welcomed everyone in the name of Jesus.[15]

But still, the missionaries walked lightly. Five years earlier, three of their colleagues had been taken captive by the communists, marched into the jungle, and had not been seen since. Another had been shot in the head in a highway ambush; his 5-month-old daughter had died as well.

As the war in Vietnam escalated, the missionaries in the city of Ban Me Thuot had made their evacuation plans. They had small bags packed. If the fighting around them became too intense, they knew just which roads they'd take.

Ban Me Thuot was a provincial capital north of Saigon, deep in the jungle of the Central Highlands. It had been a private tiger-hunting preserve of ancient Vietnamese emperors. Now, it was home to various tribes, each with its own dialect. The largest clan was the Raday people, who lived in communal groups in big, long huts suspended on log stilts above the ground for protection from predators.

Their greatest predator, however, was the one who wanted to rob their souls. One night, Bob and Marie were invited to a native ceremony. Two men wearing loincloths tied a water buffalo to a post. Then, by the light of torches, drunken, nearly-naked villagers danced around the animal with hatchets, hacking its legs and piercing it with spears, inflicting as much pain as possible because they believed that the more the animal was tortured, the more the gods of the spirit world would be pleased.

As the water buffalo writhed, the men plunged spears into its sides. They stuck a hollow bamboo tube through a spear hole into its heart. The women placed wooden bowls under the tube to catch the flood of gushing blood. Then they took the bowls throughout the village, anointing their sick people, painting their doorposts, splattering their children.

They screamed out to the darkness, "O spirits of the North, South, East, and West; spirits of the trees, rivers, rocks, and hills; spirits big and little—come, see the blood of this animal and bring us good health, and good crops, and good luck!"[16]

Bob wept. "Oh, if they only knew! If they only knew the blood of Christ cleanses from all sin!"

As Bob, Marie, and their fellow missionaries learned the Raday language and spent time among the people, more and more of them did come to know Christ. They discovered real freedom from the old ways of darkness and pain.

By the end of January 1968, Bob had finished his translation of the Bible into the local dialect. The church and school the missionaries had started were now led by a trained Raday pastor. Indigenous medical staff ran the leprosarium.

Bob was 49 years old. Humanly speaking, he had plenty of productive years ahead. However, as 1968 began, he felt glad that his main objectives—creating indigenous leadership among the Raday people in Ban Me Thuot—had been accomplished.

At the end of January, the Vietnamese people celebrated their sacred New Year, Tet. A cease-fire was in place between the People's Army of North Vietnam and the South Vietnamese and American troops. Thousands of soldiers were on leave. Civilians took to the streets in Saigon and other cities, shooting off firecrackers and fireworks as the Asian Year of the Goat ended and the Year of the Monkey began.

In the midst of the weeklong festivities, however, thousands of Viet Cong soldiers made their way into key cities in the south. Some wore civilian clothes and mingled with the populace, testing their weapons while fireworks exploded. Some wore stolen South Vietnamese army uniforms. All were heavily armed and ready to make a surprise attack.

The Tet Offensive exploded throughout South Vietnam with battles, massacres, ambushes, assassinations—and thousands of civilian casualties throughout the countryside. Tens of thousands of people were left homeless, their homes destroyed by bombings. The offensive would become one of the most famous and horrific campaigns in modern military history.

At the mission compound in Ban Me Thuot, missionaries Bob and Marie, Ed and Ruth Thompson, the father-daughter team of Leon and Carolyn Griswold, and nurses Ruth Wilting and Betty Olsen were in their homes.

The U.S. 155th Helicopter Company base was about 4 miles away. A South Vietnamese army base was just behind the compound. And Highway 14—which would turn out to be a key Viet Cong target—split right through the middle of the mission property.[17]

The missionaries had heard what was happening. But they believed that the Viet Cong who controlled the surrounding jungle would ignore them since they were noncombatants and had helped local people for years.

The missionaries also believed that God would not take them before their time. "Don't you know we are immortal until our work is done?" Ruth had written—unforgettably—to her college kids in the U.S.

On Monday night of Tet week, the missionaries fell asleep hearing the *pop-pop* of firecrackers. At 1 a.m. on Tuesday, they woke to the pops of small-arms fire and artillery. At about 3:30 a.m., communist soldiers rapped on the door of the small home that Carolyn Griswold and her father shared.

A few minutes later, there was an enormous explosion.

The Ziemers could hear moans coming from the wreckage of the Griswolds' house. North Vietnamese were coming up from the valley below them with tanks and artillery. South Vietnamese soldiers were moving across the compound grounds as their tanks rolled along the highway. Bullets were flying everywhere; to go outside would be to get caught in a deadly crossfire.

But when light dawned, Bob Ziemer and Ed Thompson ran to the ruins of the Griswold home. They desperately pulled wood and plaster aside, trying to get to Carolyn and Leon. They could hear Carolyn moaning. There was no sound from her father.

Finally, the men were able to pull away the big steel beam that lay on top of Carolyn. She had a badly broken leg and internal injuries. She was in shock. The nurses, Ruth and Betty, attended to her as Bob and Ed worked to dig Leon out. But by the time they got to him, he was dead.

The battle raged throughout Tuesday. The nurses ran through gunfire in order to get blood and plasma from the compound clinic. They had set Carolyn up on a little bed in the servants' quarters. Several wounded Raday young people from the church sought shelter there as well. Bob and Ed put up a white flag for the communists to see. They painted an SOS on an old door; they put it on top of a car to signal American pilots. They dug out the soft ground of the garbage pit behind the Thompson's house. It could serve as a make-shift bunker.

The missionaries didn't know that the nearby American helicopter base could send no help. All but two of its helicopters had been destroyed. The others were pinned down by artillery fire. Meanwhile, communist ground troops continued their assault on the South Vietnamese tanks and infantry defending their province headquarters just down the highway.

Wednesday evening, the missionaries huddled in the Ziemer home. They saw two North Vietnamese soldiers climb through a window into the Thompsons' house. A few minutes later, the whole structure blew apart, raining debris all over the compound.

Thinking the Ziemers' house would be next, the group moved to the servants' quarters. Throughout the night, the shooting intensified . . . and at about three in the morning, they decided to run for the bunker. Because of Carolyn's severe injuries, they decided that they should not try to move her again.

The Ziemers, Thompsons, and Betty and Ruth ran for the garbage pit, about 50 feet away. Bullets and shells flew all around. Raday believers from the church ran from hiding places and jumped into the bunker with them. Other wounded tribespeople were holed up all over the compound.

As dawn broke on Thursday, Ruth and Betty ran for the clinic to get more medical supplies for Carolyn. Betty shouted that she was going to get a car so she could drive Carolyn to a nearby hospital. As she swung into the driver's seat, a bullet smashed into the windshield. North Vietnamese soldiers surrounded the car, pulled her out, and dragged her away.

The Ziemers' house exploded in a huge fireball. Debris showered down on the missionaries in the bunker. Viet Cong soldiers filled the compound clearing.

All Bob knew was that he had to get his injured friends and the Raday believers out of there. Surely the soldiers would reason with him. He scrambled out of the bunker, his hands in the air, shouting to them in their own language. They responded with a barrage of gunfire; bullets crashed into Bob's head and chest. He collapsed over a low clothesline in the clearing.

Ruth ran toward the bunker as the soldiers shot her repeatedly. She fell in on top of the Thompsons and Marie Ziemer. The Viet Cong advanced. Ed raised his hands in a gesture of surrender, crying, "Mercy!"

The soldiers responded with a blast of machine-gun fire, and then lobbed grenades into garbage pit where the Americans and the Vietnamese believers huddled together.

When the Viet Cong soldiers pulled Marie from the garbage pit bunker, she was slippery with blood—her own, as well as that of her friends. The Thompsons, Griswolds, and Ruth Wilting were dead, along with the Raday believers who had taken shelter there. Betty had been taken prisoner by the Viet Cong.

Both of Marie's eardrums were punctured. She was groggy from the explosions. The soldiers forced her to her feet and propelled her forward.

Then, in the clearing just a few yards away, she saw her husband. Bob was covered with blood. The AK-47 rounds had hit his chest and upper body; he had fallen over the strong, taut cord of the compound clothesline. He was sprawled across it, hanging on that line above the ground. He was still breathing.

Marie begged the soldiers to let her go to him, to comfort him, to say good-bye. But they would not let her go. They waved their guns and forced her forward, holding her injured arms, half carrying her as she stumbled along. Weak from loss of blood, Marie kept her eyes on Bob as long as she could, until the soldiers forced her onto the highway and she could see him no more.

Bob hung over that clothesline in the mission compound, his blood pouring out on the earth, his consciousness ebbing, his breathing ragged. He would have heard, dimly, the staccato of more gunfire. Explosions. Then came a sharp rain of shrapnel, clods of earth, and a shower of stones. There were movements, rustling, his wife's sweet voice, and the shouts of the soldiers.

It all faded. Passing . . . passing . . . gone. The final beat of a once-strong heart.

Then, suddenly, in the brilliance of a thousand suns, he surely heard the joyous welcome of the golden Voice:

"Well done, good and faithful servant!"

The next day, the Viet Cong decided Marie was of no use; she was just going to die. They dumped her like a limp bag of laundry by the side of the road. Her wounds had co-agulated . . . evidently because of a brand-new slip she'd been wearing when the attacks began. It had never been washed, and there was a chemical compound in the starched fabric that had actually reacted with her blood, compressing into her wounds, staunching their flow and saving her life.

A young Raday man found Marie in the ditch. He was a Christian, one of the many young people the Ziemers had helped. He took Marie to a local hospital, where she was eventually found by Americans and airlifted back to the States.

A week or two later, a heavily armed team of U.S. military personnel escorted Christian and Missionary Alliance representatives to Ban Me Thuot. They recovered the bodies of those who had died in the compound, but Ed and Ruth Thompson, and Ruth Wilting, along with others, were still in the bunker where they had died. All three were facedown, with Ed's arm stretched over his wife as if he was trying to shield her. The pit was full of live grenades.

A Vietnamese man named Y-Ky Eban stared into the pit. He had come to know Christ as a young teenager; now, at 20, he worked at the leprosy center at Ban Me Thuot. He had been away during the Tet holiday. As Y-Ky stood at the edge of the bunker and looked down at the remains of his dead friends, he could not stop weeping.

"I heard the voice of the Lord," he says today. "I was already a believer. But that day, as I thought about the missionaries' sacrifice, I dedicated my life to serving Him without compromise."

Since it was too dangerous to try to move the missionaries, the group decided to bury them together. They carefully raked the top of the pit into a grave, erected a simple cross, and surrounded it with fresh flowers. As they wept in the ruin of the compound, a fresh breeze blew a scrap of paper across the grave.

It was a page from a blue hymnal that had been shredded in the explosions. Printed on the scorched scrap was one of those old-fashioned hymns that the missionaries used to sing in their evening services, their voices strong and joyful, blending in harmony in the jungle night:

> *Anywhere with Jesus I can safely go,*
> *Anywhere He leads me in this world below;*
> *Anywhere without Him dearest joys would fade;*
> *Anywhere with Jesus I am not afraid.*

> *Anywhere with Jesus I can go to sleep,*
> *When the darkening shadows round about me creep,*
> *Knowing I shall waken nevermore to roam;*
> *Anywhere with Jesus will be home, sweet home.*[18]

Y-Ky would remember those words many times over the next few years.

As the war dragged on, family members told him to get out of Vietnam and go to the U.S. But Y-Ky felt like he had to carry on what the missionaries had started. He continued to study the Bible and got seminary training.

In April 1977, after the end of the war and the institution of Vietnam's communist government, Y-Ky was arrested. Police threw him into a cell full of dead bodies. Guards beat him and broke his ribs. His left lung collapsed. The communists put him in a communist "re-education" camp, where he sustained many other injuries. He was held in a small cell with 26 other prisoners; they had to sleep sitting up. Sometimes the only food would be one cooked potato . . . for 27 people.

The other thing they shared—besides sleeping space and potatoes—was not known to the communists. It was Y-Ky's small, worn Bible, smuggled from prisoner to prisoner so each inmate had it for a day. The men grasped onto the words of the Bible like it was life.

And so the authorities' plans backfired. Y-Ky didn't recant his faith. He wasn't "re-educated" to the communist point of view. But many, many of his fellow prisoners did come to faith in Christ and were educated in the scriptures.

Y-Ky was released in 1981. He was still full of pain from the beatings and horror of his imprisonment , but he prayed for God's strength to forgive his enemies. He taught small groups of believers, secretly, at night. The communists still accused him of being a CIA spy, but they had grown, in an unlikely way, to respect him. Eventually, he became a leader of his denomination, with many local church leaders reporting to him.

"I lived because God allowed me to survive," he said when Ellen and I talked with him in Vietnam. "It is what Psalm 118:17 says: 'I will not die but live, and will proclaim what the Lord has done.' I am also grateful I could experience suffering for Jesus' sake; I am actually glad I can say, like the Apostle Paul, 'I bear on my body the marks of Jesus.'"[19]

Why did God allow the deaths of Bob Ziemer, the other missionaries, or the capture and eventual deaths of Betty Olsen and others, or the terrible persecution and murders of so many Vietnamese pastors and lay leaders during the war and following?[20]

We will not know the answer to such questions until we enter eternity and God reveals His mysteries. However, one thing is clear. While America's military mission in Vietnam was unresolved, God's *spiritual* mission there was not deterred by the war.

Today, in those Central Highlands near Ban Me Thuot where there were once only spirit-worshippers spilling the sacrificial blood of animals, there are hundreds of thousands of Christ-followers. The church has multiplied in some places by 500 percent;[21] many of the believers are the spiritual grandchildren and great-grandchildren of the missionaries—and others like them—who gave their lives so many years ago.

Tom Stebbins, Ruth Thompson's brother, served as a missionary in Vietnam for 20 years. He was among the last Americans evacuated from the U.S. Embassy compound in 1975. He says there were about 60,000 evangelical Christians in the country then. Today, there are a million believers, most of them from tribal areas. A Vietnamese pastor told him that his sister's heartbreaking death contributed to that growth: "When the tribal people saw that the messengers of the Gospel were willing to lay their lives down for Jesus Christ, they said this must be the truth."[22]

In March 2013, a beautiful new church was built in Ban Me Thuot with ICM's help. Pastor Y-Ky made arrangements for the Alliance missionaries' remains—which had rested in that garbage pit/bunker since he had first viewed them as a trembling 20-year-old in 1968—to be brought to Grace Church of Ban Me Thuot. The parishioners had made a landscaped area with markers for the missionaries' graves. They say that no one else will be buried there; it's a monument of remembrance for those whose sacrifice made a difference for eternity.

"They founded the church in this province," Y-Ky says about the missionaries. "Now their remains rest behind it. I want this to be a beacon for future generations, so children say, 'Oh, who are they?' And parents will tell the story: these are the people who brought the Gospel to Ban Me Thuot. *It is by their blood that we know Jesus.*"

The Rosser family in the 1950s

Dr. Bob and Janice Allen on medical mission trip to Cebu City, Philippines, 1992

Dois and Shirley's 50th Wedding Anniversary, Rosser Family, 1993

Bob hanging the "Hidden Manna" sign, February 2005

Allen Family, ACC Tournament, March 2005

Bob celebrating Grant's Wharton acceptance, on the day Bob passed away,
March 24, 2005

Archbishop Barnabas Mtokombali giving charge to Janice, Morogoro, Tanzania, 2006

Janice and Matt attend a joyous church dedication, Tanzania, 2006

Children's ministry at ICM church in Tanzania

Dois, Janice and Matt visiting congregations in rural China, 2007.

Tom and Gloria Pratt

Pastor Dick Woodward receiving ICM's Scroll Award from Dois and Janice

Rosser Family at ICM's "5000 Churches" Celebration, October 2014

Joyous welcome to a Children's Hope Center in Guatemala

Children's Hope Center in Honduras

Ellen and Maria in Guatemala, June 2015

Geof and Carolyn Stiff, Thailand, 2014

Temple prostitute, India

Rakesh, far right, and other pastors, rural India

Ellen and Janice visiting church in Upper Egypt, September 2015

Remnants of Arabic Bibles burned by radical extremists

Taking Christ's love into the villages of Moldova, 2015

Maryna and her family, husband Andrew and
Jeremiah, 2015

Kim Phuc, Trang Bang, Vietnam (source: Nick Ut)

ICM church in Kim Phuc's homeland, Trang Bang, Vietnam

Ellen, Kim Phuc and Janice at ICM Women's
Conference, Williamsburg, Virginia, March 2015

Ellen visiting with believers in DK Parthi, India

Believers dedicate their new church building in DK Parthi, India

A beautiful new church in Ban Me Thuot, Vietnam, March 2013

"It is by their blood that we know Jesus." Ban Me Thuot, Vietnam

Pastor Y-Ky, Ban Me Thuot, Vietnam

Refugee pastors celebrate the completion of MBC training, Zambia, 2015

Skull Map of Cambodia, Tuol Sleng Prison, Phnom Penh

Dois and Shirley Rosser, 2016

Janice and Shirley, 2016

CHAPTER 21

NO MORE NIGHTMARES

*"Let us ask ourselves today: are we open to
'God's surprises'?
Or are we closed and fearful before the
newness of the Holy Spirit?"*

Pope Francis

The first time I went to Vietnam years ago, I visited the Cu Chi tunnels. These are a huge network of underground warrens that surface in Ho Chi Minh City, but also run, like buried spiderwebs, throughout much of Vietnam. The tunnels served as the Viet Cong's base of operations during the Tet Offensive. Their claustrophobic passageways sheltered sleeping quarters, weapons caches, conference rooms, and supply areas. They were full of rodents, centipedes, poisonous spiders, and stinging ants.

Underground bamboo ladders led to tiny tunnel openings to the jungle floor above, trapdoors that were camouflaged by plants on the outside. Viet Cong guerillas would pop open the doors and snipe at American soldiers. They dug deep tiger traps with sharp bamboo stakes rising vertically from the bottom; soldiers would fall through the layer of leaves disguising them, and die in agony. Their fellow soldiers would rush to their rescue, only to be ambushed by the hidden Viet Cong.

Today, the horrible tunnels in Ho Chi Minh City are a tourist attraction. You can Google them and book a tour. Vendors sell souvenirs, and visitors can try their marksmanship with old M-16s at a nearby shooting range.

I declined such options. I just could not conceive of the horrors American and South Vietnamese soldiers had to endure in this place. I thought of the millions of ordinary civilians in both South and North Vietnam who had gotten caught in the middle of that terrible conflict.

Looking at those dirty, dead-end tunnels, I also thought how God had made a new way in this beautiful country. At ICM, we get to have a firsthand experience of His redeeming love.

We've been active in the southern parts of Vietnam since 1995. The 285 church projects that our partners have built there—or are building—are diverse. In Ca Ma, near the Gulf of Thailand, believers go to island churches in slender boats that look like string beans. Along the South China Sea, giggling children plop into tubs that look like silver saucers in the water, and row them to Sunday school.

In Ho Chi Minh City, ICM's big churches resound with the music of huge choirs. In the coffee plantations of the

Central Highlands, home to the Montagnard people, and the fishing areas of the South China Sea, our various structures fit the needs of the people and the types of outreach they are able to do.

Today, we're seeing more and more Christian congregations established in northern Vietnam. There are a few in Hanoi, but many among the H'mong tribal people. God has opened great doors for us among them. By early 2016, we had built or started 100 church projects in the northern part of Vietnam.

I'll never forget a worship service in the north a few years ago. I was with Dwight Pugh, a friend of ICM's ministry. Dwight had served with the U.S. military in Vietnam. Many of his wartime memories of this country were horrific and had tormented him for years.

I could see that our trip was difficult in some ways, as Dwight compared his decades-old memories with the new, great experiences we were having with our Vietnamese brothers and sisters. I knew Dwight had turned a corner when I saw him during a worship service at a church in Hanoi. He was standing between two much-shorter Vietnamese friends, his arms around them, singing an old hymn and worshipping God at the top of his lungs.

The next day, Dwight told me that he had slept the previous night in complete peace, without nightmares—the first time since he'd come home from the war.

Only God can do this. Redemption. Healing. Hope.

About 930 miles south of Hanoi, I've seen an even more powerful picture of redemption . . . ironically, in the town known for one of the world's most notorious images of wartime horror.

CHAPTER 22

THE FLAMES
SEEN AROUND
THE WORLD

"It was the fire of the bombs that burned my body,
the skill of the doctors that mended my skin.
But it took the power of God's love to heal my heart."

Kim Phuc

A 9-year-old girl runs down a village road. She is naked; she's torn off her burning clothes. Her arms are raised up in the air, desperate, as if she is trying to fly away. Her mouth is wide open in the absolute screaming anguish of fear and pain and war. Other family members are fleeing with her.

A photographer named Nick Ut captures her picture. He will win the Pulitzer Prize for that photo, which will go

136

viral in a day well before the Internet. The little girl's name is Kim Phuc.[23]

On June 8, 1972, the village of Trang Bang is the site of a confrontation between the Viet Cong and South Vietnamese forces. War photographers and journalists have come from Saigon, South Vietnam's capital, to cover the skirmish. U.S. forces are also on the ground.

A plane roars overhead, right near the Codai Temple, a landmark in the town. The temple has two brightly painted towers that reach up into the sky. Kim Phuc and other members of her family are devout Codai believers; it is a Buddhist sect. The villagers believe that the combatants will honor their religious site and not bother civilians who take cover in it.

In the terrible convergence about to take place, the photographers and American troops, seeing the approaching plane above, stand still and look up, presenting their faces to the pilot. They can see that the plane is from friendly forces, a South Vietnamese Skyraider, marked with red stripes. They know that the South Vietnamese have unwritten rules of engagement that their American advisors established early in the war. No fire is to be directed at unarmed Vietnamese, unless they are *running*, as that action indicates they are unfriendly forces.[24]

The civilians, however, do not know such rules of engagement, and so they do what comes naturally. They run . . . and the South Vietnamese Air Force pilot mistakes them, running toward shelter, for Viet Cong forces. His airplane sweeps low over the village, dropping four tumbling canisters of napalm. These drop and explode, almost in slow motion, in a deadly trail of burgeoning fire.

Developed in 1942 in a secret laboratory at Harvard University, napalm is a mixture of polystyrene and benzene, used as a thickening agent, to make jellied gasoline. It is designed to stick to human skin. While water boils at 212 degrees Fahrenheit, napalm generates temperatures of 1,500 to 2,200 degrees Fahrenheit.

So, in the famous, awful photo of that day, shot by Nick Ut, you see little Kim Phuc, running in terror away from the napalm flames. An older brother runs in front of her. Her little brother runs behind.

In the video footage shot at the same time, you see that Kim's toddler cousin, carried by her running aunt who follows, is already dead or dying, his skin coming off in dark sheets like bloody rice paper.

As the group emerges from the smoke, shocked U.S. soldiers and journalists try to help them. Troops pour water from their canteens onto Kim's sizzling skin. They can feel the heat radiating from her. They can see chunks of pink and black flesh peeling off.

All she can say, in excruciating pain, over and over, is *"Nóng quá, nóng quá!" Too hot, too hot!*

Before he delivers his film to Saigon to be developed, Nick rushes Kim Phuc to a hospital 45 almost-unbearable minutes away from Trang Bang. There, it's clear that Kim Phuc will not live. A nurse takes her to an area full of people who are either already dead or dying.

After searching for days, her relentless parents find her. They are determined that she will survive. Her father sleeps on a bench outside the hospital. Somehow, Kim keeps breathing.

The days and nights of Kim's long story, over the weeks, months, and years that followed, were excruciating. She survived nearly 20 surgical procedures and the constant, horrific pain from her burns. Photographer Nick Ut visited her until he was evacuated from the country in 1975, when Saigon fell to communist forces.

Kim returned to her home in Trang Bang. As Vietnam became a fully communist nation after the war, the government used her as a propaganda tool. She was the scarred poster child, wounded by American and South Vietnamese atrocities.

Kim survived the usual ordeals of adolescence, made far worse by her constant pain and the shame of her horrible scars. *No one will ever love me,* she thought. She considered suicide. Perhaps that might stop the pain.

One day she wandered into the American War Crimes Museum in Saigon, now christened Ho Chi Minh City. On its wall, she saw the famous photo of herself on fire; she was not even named. Evidently, to her government, she was just a nameless victim. She walked on, and came upon a library. She found a section on world religions. Incredibly, for the authorities had not yet censored them, she found books on Buddhism, Taoism, and Hinduism. Then she came upon a copy of the New Testament of the Christian Bible. She read it carefully. It was confusing to her, so at odds with the beliefs she had embraced since childhood.

At the same time, Kim became friends with a young man who was an assistant pastor at a church that was still allowed to operate in the city. He and Kim jousted for weeks in spirited discussions about faith, one's eternal destination, and real peace. Eventually, she attended a service.

There, the pastor preached about "a man who tried to do only good in his life."

Kim thought about her own devout Codai faith of her childhood. She had always tried to do the right thing. *That is me*, she thought.

The pastor continued by saying that even such an admirable person is still a "sinner" in God's eyes. Everyone falls short of God's perfection. Everyone carries burdens he or she cannot remove.

The pastor is talking to me, Kim thought. *I pray to Codai. I try to do good, and yet, I suffer. I carry a burden.*

"Let Jesus help you," the pastor called out. "Open the door to let Him in. He will come to help you. He will deliver you from your sins and bring you peace and eternal light from heaven."

It all made sense to Kim Phuc. When the pastor called for people who wanted to receive Jesus to come forward to pray with him, Kim stepped out of the pew and walked to the front of the church.

Kim's parents despaired at her change of spiritual allegiance. Meanwhile, this "girl in the picture" was still a pawn of the Vietnamese government. They monitored and controlled her life. She was forced to quit medical school in order to be available for propaganda opportunities.

In 1986, Vietnam's communist government sent her to Cuba for approved schooling. She met and fell in love with a fellow student, Bui Huy Toan. For Kim, it was a miracle that a man could love her. However, she still felt victimized, first by the napalm bombing, and second, by the communist government that viewed her as solely a propaganda tool.

In 1992, Kim and Bui Huy Toan married and honeymooned, like good communists, in Russia. But they had a plan. On a refueling stop in Newfoundland on the way back to Cuba, they got off the plane. Leaving their bags behind to avoid suspicion, they connected with Canadian officials in the airport and defected with only the clothes they were wearing.

Kim and her husband started over in Toronto. They became part of a local church, grew in their faith, and had two children. In 1997, Kim established the Kim Phuc Foundation, with the goal of providing medical and psychological help for child victims of war. She spoke to audiences around the world; she wept at the continuing atrocities raining down on innocent children who had nothing to do with the conflicts that destroyed their lives.

Kim Phuc today is a warm, ebullient woman who is quick to laugh, cry, and hug. Ellen and I met her when she spoke at a women's conference ICM sponsored in 2015. She told us that her story—which she never would have chosen—drew her to God, and has allowed her to tell people all over the world about His grace and healing.

The healing could not happen without forgiveness.

What happens when a person actually forgives those responsible for the napalm bombing that scorched her body and scarred her life? This, Kim told us:

> *Forgiveness made me free from hatred. I still have many scars on my body and severe pain most days, but my heart is cleansed. Napalm is very powerful, but faith, forgiveness, and love are much more powerful. We would not have war at all if everyone could learn how to live with true love, hope, and forgiveness. If that little girl in the picture can do it, ask yourself: Can you?*

CHAPTER 23

DECLARING HIS GLORY *THIS* DAY

"If there is one single molecule in this universe running around loose, totally free of God's sovereignty, then we have no guarantee that a single promise of God will ever be fulfilled."
R. C. Sproul

The Buddhist temple where Kim and her family tried to hide from the warplanes is still intact today, its twin towers rising into the blue sky. The family noodle shop that Kim's parents ran during the war is still there. Old photos are on the walls, including the famous image of the burned villagers running down the road. When I walked on that same road, I could imagine the thick plumes of smoke and fire, the children running out of the flames.

142

But there is an addition to the town, one that wasn't there during the days of the Vietnam War, when there were *no* Christians in Trang Bang.

It is a beautiful church on the main street of the town. Dr. Minh Dang, our church-building partner in Vietnam, had submitted an application for a church here. A church in Ohio agreed to fund it. What we didn't know was that the church was a direct answer to Kim Phuc's years of prayer, after her conversion, for her home village.

Kim didn't know the first person to follow Christ in Trang Bang. He came to know Jesus long after Kim had left the area. He is an elderly, thoughtful man named Van Thanh Vo. Years ago, he was the village witch doctor. As a young man, Van had given himself over to what he calls "dark powers." He swore a terrible oath of allegiance. They enabled him to foresee the future. He practiced animal sacrifice. People came to him to heal their children.

Then, while Van was living in Saigon in the late 1980s, his own 11-year-old daughter became seriously ill. He could not make her well, even though he called on the devil for help. His daughter went with a friend to a church in Saigon that ICM had built. The pastor prayed for her. Her disease disappeared.

Van continued to practice his occult rituals, but he was curious about Christianity. He got a Bible from a friend and read the New Testament. Months went by. He would not make a change. His friend told him, "Don't be hard-hearted! You *know* the power of God!"

Finally acknowledging his inner desperation, Van found the pastor of the church in Saigon. "Please!" he asked him, desperately. "Please pray for me!" The pastor put his hands on

Van and prayed fervently for him. Van poured out his fears and sins from his years of living in darkness. He prayed for the Light of Jesus Christ to fill his heart. He was baptized.

Van moved back to his hometown of Trang Bang around 1988. He told all his relatives about Christ. They saw his new joy, freedom, and the lightness in his step. The heavy burdens he had carried for years were gone.

Many in the village came to faith in Christ. They met in the former witch doctor's home, and as their numbers grew, Van moved his family to the back corner of his property, to make more room for the house church. The congregation prayed for a building. They met our partner Minh when he traveled through their area, and Minh submitted the application for ICM to build a church.

Van donated his land for the church building, and in December 2011, after much prayer, many hardships, and innumerable hassles with the local communist authorities, the Trang Bang church was completed. "God answered our prayers by sending ICM," Van says.

Today, that church is planting daughter congregations. Children are coming to know Jesus through all kinds of creative outreaches. Evangelistic teams go out into surrounding areas every week. Kim Phuc's younger sister is the church treasurer. And her younger brother, the little boy from the famous photo of the napalm bombing, is a deacon.

This younger brother's name is Phan Thanh Phuc. He is a short man with a round face and a huge smile. He was 6 years old on that day in 1972; in the famous photo, he is in the background, eyeing the terrible black smoke behind him.

"My hair was on fire," he says today. "I don't remember much of anything. Just the *'boom, boom, boom!'* and the darkness, and the chaos."

Phan was not burned as horribly as his older sister. But the hideous day burned a hole in his soul. "I grew up hating the Americans, hating a world where such things could happen to children," he says. "I worshipped Buddha . . . but I had no peace. Only hatred and darkness." He tried to dull his pain with anger, alcohol, and cynicism.

Kim prayed for her brother for years, and in 2002, as a middle-aged man, Phan finally opened his life to Jesus. He says that the power of darkness chained him for a long time. "I could not receive love. I could not really give love. Love without forgiveness is not full love, but once I knew God's forgiveness for me, then I could forgive and love others."

Ellen and I sat with Phan to watch the iconic black-and-white video of the napalm bombing that a reporter shot on June 8, 1972, when the young children ran out of the dark plumes of smoke and fire. It was almost unfathomable to juxtapose the terrified little boy in the photo with the smiling man beside us, and hard to connect that long-ago terrible day in Trang Bang with the peace in that place today.

"You know," Phan told us, "that video is full of pain and horror. But now, when I look at it, I know God allowed it. He used it to start the process of leading us all to Him. And I know He kept me alive *that* day so I can declare His glory *this* day."

CHAPTER 24

RADIOACTIVE SOIL, HOLY GROUND

"The desert and the parched land will be glad;
the wilderness will rejoice and blossom.
Like the crocus, it will burst into bloom;
it will rejoice greatly and shout for joy."

Isaiah 35:1–2

Though the Iron Curtain fell in the paradigm-changing days of the late 1980s, we have found that ministry in the former Soviet Union has been indelibly marked by 70 years of communism.

That fact is clear in Ukraine.

In 1972, construction workers of the former Soviet Union commenced a landmark project: the government's first nuclear power plant in Ukraine. It was a symbol of the regime's peaceful atomic energy program, a state-of-the-art nuclear power plant with four huge reactors. Now, it is well-known that the plant's design was inherently flawed. Back then, it was the pride of Moscow.

A similarly ambitious town called Pripyat was built near the reactor for the plant's scientists, workers, security troops, and their families. It was a grid of streets full of modern shops, restaurants, department stores, government buildings, a hotel, and homes. The Soviet Palace of Culture was full of entertainment for Pripyat's 50,000 industrious citizens. There was a giant Ferris wheel and a sports complex with sports fields, bumper cars, and other entertainment. Commissioned in 1977, the shiny new plant and its brave new town were both bustling prototypes of modern life and efficiency in the USSR.

Though Pripyat was the official residence for the families, the plant is best known by the name of another city, one about 8 miles south of the reactor.

Chernobyl.

In the predawn hours of April 26, 1986, engineers were conducting a systems test in Reactor Number 4. When extremely hot nuclear fuel rods were lowered into the plant's cooling water, a huge amount of scalding steam billowed forth, creating more reactivity in the nuclear core. Workers—who had disabled the automatic shutdown mechanisms, in violation of safety regulations—frantically tried to close it all down.

Instead, there was a massive, exponentially more powerful, spike in power. A reactor vessel blew up, there were a series of steam explosions, and graphite from the reactor hit the air, causing it to ignite.

The resulting fire was like a scene from Judgment Day. Reactor 4 melted down. The raging plumes of flame spewed deadly radioactive fallout all over the area, and the particles drifted over large swaths of the western Soviet Union and Europe. Plant workers died immediately, and others eventually passed away from acute radiation sickness.

It took Soviet officials 40 hours to absorb the scale of their catastrophe and order the full evacuation of Pripyat. Within 3 hours, the town's 50,000 men, women, and children fled their homes, never to return. Many were already vomiting and suffering from strange, strong headaches.

Today, if you were able to stroll the ghost city's streets, you would see its 1970s-era Ferris wheel, no longer shiny, covered with thick, gray dust. The bumper cars and sports complex of the glorious Palace of Culture, with its wrecked Soviet propaganda murals, look like props from an apocalyptic horror movie. The once-charming sidewalk café, with its stained-glass windows, is full of broken glass. The floor of the post office is littered with letters that will never be delivered. A rusty bicycle is propped against the wall of the tomblike hospital. A headless mannequin is the only customer in a dead department store.

Outside the town, the surrounding woodlands died. The region is now called the "Red Forest" since the radioactive trees turned a dull, rusty color. The radioactive fallout zone is about 1,004 square miles. The ghost towns of Pripyat and Chernobyl became part of the "Exclusion Zone," an "Area of Absolute (Mandatory) Resettlement."

The ground zero zone of the explosion will be off-limits until there's a new heaven and a new earth. In 1986, the melted reactor was encased in a steel and concrete sarcophagus, like a giant dead thing.

Who would go to a blighted place like this?

Several years ago, a group of students in a seminary in Kiev asked their professor what was going on in Chernobyl. They had heard that the government had invited people to come back to the area, and many families, hungry for home, had returned to the forest around Chernobyl.

Do they have churches? the students wondered. *Who is helping them with their physical and spiritual needs in that desolate place?*

With their professor's blessing, the students rounded up a group of like-minded young people. They started traveling on the weekends from Kiev to Chernobyl. They found that many people had taken the Soviet government's less-than-helpful advice in the decades since the explosion: authorities had told people that drinking plenty of alcohol would help them resist radiation sickness. The government had also provided for many, many women to get abortions . . . in spite of the fact that the number of birth defects turned out to be much lower than expected.

Many of the resettled townspeople were inveterate alcoholics, living on vodka. Many were consequently abusive or had left their families. In addition, since Chernobyl is close to the Russian border, many Russian soldiers would engage with Ukrainian women, but never marry them. Most homes are all female: there is typically an elderly grandmother, or babushka, her daughter, and her daughter's children, all crammed together in a makeshift hovel.

The seminarians began to make friends with the people they met. People began to get interested in the hope of the Gospel . . . but it was slow going.

One day, the seminary group had traveled to Chernobyl in two cars. One of the leaders, a young man named Daniil

Muzychenko, was in one vehicle. His sister Alina was in the other. As they sped through the rutted roads home to Kiev that night, the sister's car ran off the road and hit a tree. When the brother rushed to her car, he found his sister was dead.

From that terrible night onward, Daniil was overcome by grief every time he traveled the road to Chernobyl. He couldn't help reliving the accident and the loss of his sister. He was tempted to quit, to just work in Kiev or someplace like it, but he knew the people in the village were counting on him. He knew that his sister would want him to keep going back. And he knew that God had distinctly called him to bring healing and hope to Chernobyl's toxic ground.

Daniil graduated from seminary, and today, he and his wife, Luba, live in Chernobyl. Daniil pastors the church there. (The congregation used to meet in an old log cabin, but now they have a beautiful new building, built in partnership with ICM.) They've opened a coffee shop as a place of outreach to young people, with a bakery to give people jobs and disciple them at the same time. The locals are pleasantly shocked that they actually use honest weights—it's a refreshing change from "business as usual." When bread deliveries from Kiev stopped, the mayor asked them to provide bread for the local school. Meanwhile, Daniil and his congregation faithfully provide the Bread of Life to all who are spiritually hungry.

CHAPTER 25

MYSTERIES FROM THE FIRE

"God uses broken things. It takes broken soil to produce a crop, broken clouds to give rain, broken grain to give bread, broken bread to give strength. It is the broken alabaster box that gives forth perfume. It is Peter, weeping bitterly, who returns to greater power than ever."

Vance Havner

We've been working for years in other parts of Ukraine, like Bucha, a small city about 16 miles from Kiev. A young girl named Maryna was born there in the mid-1980s. She lived a quiet life with her parents and two sisters.

One evening when Maryna was 18 months old, her mother was cooking a traditional Ukrainian dish. A shiny pot of oil simmered on the simple stove. Curious, Maryna toddled to the cooking area, reached up, and tipped the pot. Almost a liter of boiling oil spilled over her upturned face and chest.

Maryna remembers nothing of that horrible night. Her sister, who was 3 or 4 at the time, recalls screaming, chaos, and tears.

Maryna's parents did everything they could, but their income was less than the equivalent of $250 a year. Maryna has one hazy memory of her mother carrying her to the operating room for a surgery.

She lived, though at times she wished she had not.

Much of her facial skin had melted. Her nose, ears, and lips were gone. Her teeth were exposed in a grimace. The pain was terrible, but the psychological torment was worse. As she grew older, Maryna would cover her disfigured face with scarves. Though she had never heard of Kim Phuc, she knew the same shame and self-disgust that Kim had felt. Boys would tease her: "You're a monster! No one will ever love you! You'll never get married!"

In the late 1990s, my father traveled to Ukraine for the dedication of a church that ICM had built in Bucha, near Kiev. Dad saw a young teenager swathed in scarves. He asked ICM's partner, Pastor Viktor Kulbich, about her. The pastor gently asked Maryna to remove her facial covering. Dad's heart broke over the damage done to this innocent girl. He thought of his own three daughters, and what life would be like for us if we were injured and disfigured like Maryna.

Eventually, through the help of all kinds of compassionate people, ICM was able to arrange for her to come to the U.S. for medical care, along with her older sister, Sasha. By then, Maryna had just turned 16.

"I was really excited," she says today. "I didn't speak any English. I had no idea, really, what to expect. But I listened to everything, tried to take it all in, and somehow, God gave me understanding."

Maryna and Sasha lived with a Christian family near ICM's office and got involved with a local church. Maryna was baptized. She endured many, many painful surgeries performed by compassionate surgeons who donated their services.

Maryna got her GED, went to college, and worked in various jobs. She got involved with the singles' ministry in her church. She made friends there, including Andrew Vanderjagt, whom she met on a missions trip to New York.

One summer day, the singles class had an outing at a local pool. Everyone was swimming, splashing, and laughing. Maryna wasn't able to swim because of a tracheotomy wound, but she was sitting on the edge of the pool, watching everyone.

Suddenly, she saw one of the guys in the shallow water, face up. His skin was purple. It was Andrew. In the fun chaos, no one else had noticed.

Maryna jumped into the water, reached down, and pulled Andrew above the surface, calling for help. Andrew was twitching and shaking; he was having a seizure. The lifeguard and others jumped in. They pulled him out and called an ambulance.

Andrew survived. And Maryna's heroism caught his attention. He began e-mailing her. They became closer friends. They went ice skating and out for coffee.

"I'd never been in a relationship with a boy before," Maryna says. "I liked him. But I didn't know if he liked me."

One night in January 2008, Andrew invited Maryna to the beach. He had set up an elaborate scavenger hunt; she found notes taped to the pier, hidden under rocks, and in the sand marked with a stick. The last note indicated that Andrew wanted to ask her something.

"He wanted to see if I would be 'in courtship' with him," Maryna says. "It was so beautiful. I had been praying for God to bring a man into my life who would love me in spite of the scars. And here he was!"

Maryna and Andrew were married in 2009. Their wedding pictures show a glowing bride, full of joy. No more scarves covering her face in shame, but a bridal veil framing her long, strawberry blond hair and a huge smile. Today, Maryna and Andrew have a happy little boy and are expecting a little girl.

When I hold Maryna's bright-eyed, chunky toddler, Jeremiah, I see reflections of the sweet-faced toddler Maryna must have been before boiling oil changed her life. It's a mystery . . . if not for the accident, Maryna never would have come to the U.S., never would have met Andrew, and Jeremiah wouldn't have been born. God is always at work, if we have eyes to see. He can bring new life, joy, and hope, even out of fire.

"I don't know what my life would have been like without International Cooperating Ministries and Mr. Rosser," Maryna says. "I gave my life to Jesus in my church in Ukraine that ICM built. Without ICM, I wouldn't have had spiritual or physical hope—and I wouldn't have become the person I am today."

CHAPTER 26

BURIED TREASURE

"The way you store up treasure in heaven is by investing in getting people there."

Rick Warren

"The kingdom of heaven is worth infinitely more than the cost of discipleship, and those who know where the treasure lies joyfully abandon everything else to secure it."

D. A. Carson

Another former Soviet satellite, Moldova, is not far from where Maryna grew up. We partner there with a group called Bible Mission International. This ministry provides humanitarian aid, outreach, and church planting in about nine of the 15 former Soviet republics: Russia, Belarus, Moldova, Ukraine, Kazakhstan, Kyrgyzstan, Uzbekistan, Tajikistan, and Turkmenistan. Many of these states are Muslim-controlled, and because of security issues, we are unable to write the stories of what God is doing in them at this time.

BMI's leader in the region is Paul Hagelgans. He is originally from Kazakhstan, but lives in Frankfurt now. He is a visionary, unstoppable man of God.

Paul brings teams of builders and engineers from churches in Frankfurt each summer, so when the Moldovan believers are working on their houses of prayer during the winters, the shell and roof are already in place, protecting them from the elements.

When visiting there recently, the men from our ICM team had a unique opportunity to work side-by-side with the Germans, constructing a church for the Moldovans. It was a taste of the cooperation, fellowship, and unity of heaven . . . except that in heaven, we'll be able to understand each other's languages!

While the men worked on the building, the women went to poor homes in the area, bringing food. We were led by Bietta, who serves with BMI. Bietta grew up as a committed communist in the former East Germany, became a Christian during her university years, excelled in languages, and now serves as a translator.

Our little group picked our way along dirt roads lined with broken stone walls. We came to a small, gray village. The first home was built of stone. There was a little vegetable garden in the back. As we were invited in, we saw a tiny alcove, then a room just large enough to hold two twin beds.

We met a woman with strawberry blond hair. Wearing a worn terry cloth bathrobe, she was cradling her son, who was naked. We were told he was 10 years old and suffered from cerebral palsy. The bare mattress of the bed was saturated with his urine. The mom was trying to pull a sheet over her withered son.

My heart broke for them. I sat down on the ruined bed and touched the mom gently on the shoulder. Bietta translated for me as I tried to tell her how I understood how hard her circumstances must be, how I admired her for caring so tenderly for her son each day. Her husband had left a long time ago, and she lived in this hovel with her mother. The two women were trying their best to provide for the disabled son, though they had no resources.

I held the woman and prayed for her. We left the bundle of food that we had brought and noted her home for a follow-up visit from the sisters and brothers from the church.

There was a similar situation at the next small house: a grandmother, her daughter, and small children all living together. The daughter had lived there ever since her alcoholic husband stopped beating her long enough to set their house on fire. Miraculously, she and her children had escaped.

Her mother's home was dark and cramped, with a dirt floor. The glass from the windowpanes had shattered long ago, perhaps around the time that her drunken husband had left her. The kids had no shoes, matted hair, and dirty clothes. There was one double bed pad on the floor for everyone, with a burning fire pit next to it. Soot was everywhere.

We gave the women our food basket and presented the little boys with Matchbox cars. They were so excited, you would have thought we had given them iPhones. Then we prayed for the mom as her eldest son, perhaps 10 or 11, stood next to her. It was clear that he saw himself as the man of the family. He began to weep. Then, embarrassed, he turned away.

This boy, as well as his siblings and friends, are the kids for whom we build Hope Centers. There, they can receive the things they lack at home, like plenty of good food, games, schooling, and Bible teaching. They begin to learn about

Jesus, and the way of hope, new life, responsibility, and the power of God. They learn that life is about so much more than the anger, abuse, and regrets that come at the bottom of an empty vodka bottle. They will become a new generation of Christians in the region.

In a Moldovan village called Carpineni, a former communist youth camp is today the site of a new Christian camp. It's another example of ICM's partnership with Bible Mission International. Back in Soviet times, it was a place where young people could practice parade drills, play sports, and learn the doctrines of Marx and Engels. After the collapse of communism, the camp collapsed as well. The soccer field was taken over by wild vegetation. The pond was covered in thick scum. The buildings were stained and falling down.

Now, ICM is partnering with BMI to renovate that camp. It is called Camp Torch of Faith, and the former propaganda place for dead ideologies is now a center to train the next generation of Christian leaders in that part of Moldova. There is already a full-time pastor who had actually started working in the ruined camp some years ago, but had to stop because of safety issues. A thousand kids have already received Jesus through his work. Once completed in 2017, the camp will host and train 2,000 kids every year.

A dynamic young pastor named Ruslan Meleştean directs BMI's work in Moldova, which is the poorest country in Europe. He tells the story of one church building and complex that ICM built for local believers, who received a financial boost in a way they had not anticipated.

In Burlacu, a village in the approximate middle of nowhere, perhaps 300 miles south of Chernobyl, the believers had been worshipping for decades in a rickety 100-year-old building. It was heavily damaged by the area's notoriously heavy winter snows, and government authorities had deemed it unsafe. The pastor—who was also a teacher at the local school—had no idea how his congregation could build a new church or how they could fund it. Through Ruslan, ICM came into the story, and the pastor could not wait to get started.

He had to travel several hours to Chisinau, Moldova's capital city, to secure the necessary construction approvals. He assumed that getting the signatures was just a formality, so he told his congregants to go ahead and start digging the foundation.

The design was an L-shaped building, with one wing to be the place of worship, and the other to serve as a Hope Center for the area's many needy children. Some of the hardier church members started enthusiastically digging the rocky soil with shovels. They had no construction equipment, but soon had made great progress toward excavating the foundation area.

Meanwhile, the gray-suited authorities in Chisinau peered solemnly at the design plans for the building. The pastor felt his stomach twist with worry as they shook their heads. They would be beneficent and still sign the documents, they told him . . . *if* he would move the church foundation 3 meters to the right.

The pastor knew better than to argue with the bureaucrats. He jumped in his dilapidated vehicle and careened back home. He leapt out at the construction site and ran to his friends, who were still digging away.

"Brothers!" he shouted. "STOP!"

He explained the dubious wisdom of the big-city bureaucrats. There was a lot of grumbling. But, in the end, the exhausted church members started over and dug away. Eventually, in a hole at the corner of the new foundation location, their shovels struck something hard. It turned out to be a rusty, iron box.

They hauled it out of the hole, pried it open, and stared in disbelief at its contents: a pile of old gold coins.

They rushed their treasure to the old church building, cleaned the coins, and eventually realized that they were imperial gold rubles from the 1890s, commissioned by the last czar of Russia, Nicholas II. They were worth about $60,000—a *huge* amount of money in Moldova.

The workers who had found the cache reacted, at first, with default human nature. "We're rich! See how God has blessed us! Let's divide these coins between ourselves."

The pastor stepped in. "Brothers! This is God's money for the ministry. If you try to keep it, Satan will use it to cause awful division among us."

The others agreed. They turned the money over to the church treasurer.

About the same time, the pastor's cell phone rang. It was the authorities in Chisinau. They acknowledged they had made a mistake in their initial calculations. The building's original placement was correct, and they should now move the foundation 3 meters back to the left.

The pastor and his people just laughed. If not for the bureaucrats' error, they never would have found their hidden treasure. They used the money to buy additional land next door to their original plot, and to build a beautiful complex for prayer, the teaching of God's Word, and ministry to the children and everyone else in their community.

The complex was completed and dedicated to God in 2014. It is flourishing. And that faithful pastor was able to resign from his school-teaching job, in order to concentrate full-time on nurturing his hardworking flock.

And, yes, all the other pastors in the area have furiously been digging up their land as well, looking for crates of buried treasure.

CHAPTER 27

TRIBAL BROTHERS, GOSPEL WARRIORS

"We are preaching hope, standing on the bones of the past."
Bishop John Rucyahana

Many of the places where ICM serves are villages or remote towns known to few people on the planet, but well loved by God. Other locations are well-known—infamous, in fact—because of their troubled history of war, genocide, violence, or religious persecution.

Rwanda is one such place.

Like many African nations, Rwanda had its history of upheaval, civil war, and clan conflict between its major tribes, the majority Hutus and the minority Tutsis. But in this beautiful green "land of a thousand hills," the "Switzerland of Africa," horror took hold in April 1994.

It began with the mysterious missile attack of the presidential plane as it prepared to land in the capital city, killing Rwanda's president and the president of neighboring Burundi, who was traveling with him. Already-prepared Hutu militias burst into action, blaming members of the minority Tutsi tribe, whom they called "cockroaches," for the assassination.

The marauders—murderous groups of young men wielding machetes—also killed members of their own Hutu tribe who wanted peace and tolerance, and anyone else who stood in their way. Radio broadcasts fanned the flames of violence and hatred. Announcers advised citizens to stay in their homes . . . where they would be easier to isolate and kill. The moderate acting president of the country, a Hutu, named Agathe Uwilingiyimana, was tracked down and murdered, along with her husband. Other moderate government officials were assassinated. Civilians who sought sanctuary in churches were massacred.

Militia members set up roadblocks, where they demanded identity cards. If your tribal designation—or the way you looked—did not please them, you would be dragged out of your car and murdered right on the roadway. Students at suspect schools were killed. Babies and toddlers were cut into pieces. People who had known one another for years turned on each other. To put it in U.S. terms, neighbors you might have waved at while walking the dog in your neighborhood or acquaintances you chatted with in the grocery store—those people came to your house to kill you.

"It was as if satanic forces were unleashed on our country," one pastor said. "The killers were drunk on blood." They slaughtered United Nations peacekeepers. Other countries, including the United States, stood back. And in the end, over the course of 3 months, nearly a million Rwandans were killed by other Rwandans. Hutus killed Tutsis, and in a horrific backlash, Tutsis killed Hutus. Death was everywhere.

It is still difficult for Westerners to analyze Rwanda's politics and history in a way that rings true with all Rwandans. The fact that the West stood by and did not intervene is a blight on the administration that served during that time— one for which the president felt deep regret—and a shame for many Americans.

Today, Rwanda is a bright spot in Africa. Its leaders have brought it forward in terms of its economy, infrastructure, and education. Its global competitiveness rating is first in East Africa, third in Africa as a whole.

The genocide is memorialized in national museums to remind the world and Rwanda not to forget. A generation of 20-somethings has taken its place in society. They are the children of rape. Many perpetrators have served decades in prison . . . and many have escaped human justice. The key to Rwanda's future is in its citizens' forgiveness of the past.

In this environment, ICM's work goes forward, led by two men who come from the tribes that once killed one another.

Ananie Bagaragaza is Tutsi; Juvenal Twagirayezu is Hutu. Like most of their fellow citizens today, they prefer to be called "Rwandans" rather than be known by their tribal origins. They both lost many loved ones in the terrible days of the genocide. But today, they work together as brothers to build churches all over their country. If you spend any amount of time with them to hear their stories, you'll laugh and drink a lot of very good Rwandan coffee.

During the genocide, Ananie was a national church leader. He was able to cross over to the Democratic Republic of the Congo and hide there from the gangs that went from house to house, killing his people. Many of his family members ran from their homes to hide in the bush. They tried to survive in the jungle. But eventually, they were dragged from their hiding places and killed. The pastor who had led Ananie to faith in Jesus, his spiritual father, was hacked to death on the road, his body left in the dust.

Juvenal was in high school during the genocide. He hid in the bush for a month, somewhere near the border between Rwanda and Tanzania. He had no idea what was happening to his family, but when he came out from hiding, he learned that his loved ones had all been killed in the aftermath of the initial slaughter, at the hands of Tutsis avenging their tribal brothers.

Juvenal says his Christian faith was nominal at the time. He went through the motions of following his parents in faith, attending the Anglican Church. After the murderous spring of 1994, though, he didn't have it within himself to forgive anyone for the violence that had destroyed his family and his country. He was angry, miserable, bitter, and hopeless.

Eventually, Juvenal found the intimate faith he had known only formally. He began to know Jesus personally. Christ taught him how to forgive. He opened himself to be used in God's service, however God willed.

Our Rwandan partners are particularly grateful for the solid teachings of ICM's Mini Bible College, and the solid way ICM constructs standout church buildings.

First, the need for good biblical instruction is paramount. Bible teaching in past generations wasn't always centered in the truths of the scriptures. Ananie and Juvenal point out that Rwanda was allegedly 95 percent Christian at the time of the genocide. But many Rwandans' faith was just a veneer. They did not know the Bible well enough for it to serve as a restraint to tribal violence. When evil came, many so-called Christians participated as much as anyone else.

Nor would anyone today be able to forgive the heinous crimes of the past without the actual indwelling of the Holy Spirit. "Forgiveness is only possible if people are united in the Word of God," says Juvenal. "I should know."

So clear, fundamental biblical teaching is fundamental. Toward that end, there are 341 groups currently studying MBC in Rwanda.

Second, since Rwanda's government is intent on advancing their small country and building everything in it with excellence, ICM's churches there are particularly important. Christians who do not have a building are looked at askance by authorities, and villagers don't respect a church that has no permanent meeting place. "In Rwanda," Ananie explains, "a church isn't considered real unless it has a building."

Geof Stiff visited Rwanda a few years ago. As his group stopped at a beautiful church orphanage, Geof went over to the nearby home of one of the church elders. It was a mud hut, about 10 feet by 15 feet. There was a tarp stretched out from the top of the hut to a tree. Under its shade, there were about a dozen adults gathered for Bible study. The pastor was listening to a Mini Bible College teaching in African English on his solar-powered audio player. He'd absorb a section, then turn off the player and painstakingly translate it into the local language, Kinyarwanda, for the group. The group members would burst into animated discussion, asking questions and talking about life situations in which they could apply what they were learning from the Bible.

"It was beautiful," Geof says today, "a microcosm of what MBC is facilitating all over the world. And since that visit, MBC has been translated into Kinyarwanda, so people who don't speak African English can now understand its teaching for themselves!"

In our desire to blanket whole nations with Bible-teaching churches, we usually try to build a church every 25 miles in a given country. However, since Rwanda is compact, slightly smaller than the state of Maryland, we decided to build churches—62 so far—every 12½ miles across its length and breadth.

One of our great partners in the U.S. has been the Church of the Holy Spirit in Roanoke, Virginia. It's pastored by Quigg Lawrence, a passionate Anglican bishop who has long been a friend of ICM.

Bishop Quigg's church is under the authority of the Rwandan Anglican Church. It makes sense, then, that he and his congregation have focused on communities in Rwanda they can help. It is a two-way relationship in which Americans can bring resources to provide for needs in Rwanda, even as they are learning much from the Rwandans about humility, resourcefulness, and prayer.

Quigg's church has connected with people who have been cut off from the world for a long time.

They live on an island, Nkombo, in Lake Kivu, the big body of water between Rwanda and the Democratic Republic of the Congo. Nkombo is 20 miles long, 3 to 5 miles wide, and populated by a forgotten people group. They are desperately poor. They live on what they can catch in the lake, tiny fish about the size of an adult's pinkie finger. They speak a different language than the Rwandans on the mainland.

Their population swelled after the genocide, when 20,000 refugees—mostly malnourished, traumatized children—were relocated there.

The first time Quigg visited Nkombo, his heart broke. The people were isolated physically, emotionally, and spiritually. The children had no chance to grow up, live, and thrive. They were stuck in a dead end unless God's people came to them and brought the tangible love of Jesus.

So that's what happened.

Today, on Nkombo Island, there are two church Hope Centers; one is feeding 705 children, the other 400. As I write, Quigg's congregation has raised money to build a biblically based school for 800 students. They have built two churches; the largest includes office space for Compassion International, which is running three projects on the island, serving 750 children. The kids are full of joy and hope; the adults can't believe how God has blessed them with an invigorated community.

"Nkombo Island is being transformed from a polygamous island of starvation and misery to an island of the Kingdom of God," Quigg says. "Two and a half years ago, the children looked half dead, in tatters, hungry, unable to read. Now they are healthy, in uniform, learning to read and write, and learning the Bible. You can feel and smell and almost taste HOPE!

"Building churches gives us the best chance to win people to Jesus, and also to disciple them," Quigg continues. "A church changes a community in so many ways, not because of the building, but because of what comes through it: discipleship! Seeing what God has done through ICM on Nkombo Island is like seeing Acts 2:42 come alive."

As that passage says, the followers of Jesus "devoted themselves to the apostles' teaching and to fellowship, to the breaking of bread and to prayer." The new believers of Nkombo are doing the same thing, studying the Word of God, supporting one another in real biblical community, breaking bread together, and relying on God's power in fervent prayer.

To finish off the picture, I would only add the end of Acts 2:47, for this is what is happening all over Rwanda, that beautiful green land that was once best known for murder and death . . . now full of new life and hope:

"*. . . And the Lord added to their number daily those who were being saved.*"

CHAPTER 28

THE CALL AND THE COST

*"Then I saw thrones, and the people sitting on them
had been given the authority to judge. And I saw the souls
of those who had been beheaded for their testimony about
Jesus and for proclaiming the word of God."*
Revelation 20:4

The world is a dangerous place for Christians today. My
faith in Christ is challenged—and humbled—every day
by the courage and commitment of our partners and friends
in the field. Many are facing unprecedented persecution.

The religious freedom group Open Doors reports that
around the world, 322 Christians are killed for their faith
every month, and 722 others are victims of violence. Every

month, 214 churches and properties owned by Christians are destroyed.

Bulk statistics regarding persecution are one thing. Hearing the story of one family those statistics describe is another.

Pastor Yesudass had been a pastor in Karnataka state in southern India for years. Like other Indian pastors, he was accustomed to threats from the elders in his village. "How can you be Christian?" they would shout at him. "It's a foreign religion. A Western religion! India is Hindu! If you don't stop, something very bad will happen."

Pastor Yesudass kept preaching. His congregation had about 250 people, of whom 150 were baptized members. He and his wife had four children and were raising their three boys and one girl to know Christ and to share His Gospel.

After the evening service one Sunday in the summer of 2013, their third son, Paul Kumar, went to a nearby park to play with friends. He was 13 years old.

At about 7 p.m., Pastor Yesudass got a phone call telling him his son had been found at the railroad crossing. He and his wife ran to the railroad track . . . and there was their beloved son—dead. He was wearing the black T-shirt with a cross and white pants that he had left church in. His body was positioned so part of him was on one side of the rail, and his head was on the other. He had been beheaded.

The police concluded that Paul Kumar had been killed elsewhere and then laid out symbolically. Perhaps, they said, his murder was part of a tribal sacrifice ritual; perhaps he had been killed as a warning to the pastor and his wife.

After their son's murder, Pastor Yesudass and his family bravely kept up the good work in their village. But they were devastated by their loss. Paul Kumar had been a devout boy, planning to go to Bible school after his high-school graduation in order to serve the Lord full-time. The district chairman of Pastor Yesudass's denomination and his colleagues were able to buy land in order to build a church in memory of Paul Kumar. At this writing, however, government authorities have not yet granted permission for the church to be built.

I can't imagine the challenges brothers like Pastor Yesudass face every day. Sadly, in terms of persecution, his situation is the norm rather than the exception in backward areas of the countries where we work.

Much of India is firmly first world. If your computer has an issue and you call the help line, you usually end up talking with some wonderful person in New Delhi who will shepherd you through your technology problems. India's cities are full of high-earning, highly educated, sophisticated young people. Indian cinema is a booming business. Indian doctors, engineers, and scientists are at the forefront of their fields.

Nevertheless, about half of the nation's citizens—roughly 700 million people, about twice the population of the United States—live in rural villages that feel far more like the Dark Ages than the Information Age. Illiteracy and ignorance are common. Many communities are ruled by councils that dispense "justice" for those who violate Hindu standards, as in the notorious recent case when a young tribal woman in West Bengal was gang-raped by village elders and other men as punishment for seeing a Muslim suitor.

Women are often abused in other ways. Witch doctors manipulate the fearful. Though the practice is officially against the law, "*devadasi*," or temple prostitutes, still exist. Five thousand to 10,000 preteen girls are sold each year for this purpose, forced into the service of the goddess Yellamma.[25, 26] The young girls are considered one with the goddess. Men come to roadside temples and pay for sex, believing that if they have relations with the girl, they gain favor with the goddess.

Another old, sinister practice is also at work in some places. Once I was in an Indian village and met four beautiful, giggling girls, about 9 years old. I asked the local pastor about them, and he told me that it was common for poor families to poison their baby daughters. That way, they don't have to raise them and can try again for the baby boy they really want. The pastor had "bought" these girls as newborns, for $2 each, and brought them home. He and his wife have raised them as their own.

Again, such practices are not the case all over India . . . but cruelty, devaluation of women, fear, and ancient ignorance are hallmarks of the places where our partners work, not just in India, but in many other parts of the modern world as well.

Consider the island of Zanzibar, off the coast of East Africa. ICM has built 11 churches and a Hope Center on the main island there. It's an exotic place with a colorful and troubled history.

The center of Zanzibar is Stone Town, a trade center with Swahili and Islamic influences. The sultans of nineteenth-century Zanzibar developed trade with the ruling Arab elites of their day. Cloves, cinnamon, nutmeg, black pepper, and other spices, as well as ivory, were precious goods. There was another, less precious, trade commodity: human beings.

Zanzibar was the Swahili Coast's center for the slave trade with the Middle East. In the mid-nineteenth century, as many as 50,000 slaves passed annually through the port.

The reigning sultan encouraged the trade. Corrupt African chiefs would sell their villagers to slave traders, who brought them in stinking ship holds to Zanzibar. The slaves would then be sold for huge profits in its capital slave market.

An Anglican church in the capital commemorates the trade's horrors. Its site used to be Zanzibar's main slave block. The church chancel is inlaid with red marble to commemorate their blood. Statues are everywhere, depicting the Africans in their suffering. They were chained in a dark cavern beneath the block. You can see the steel hooks in the dank walls that once secured their chains.

The holding pit was designed in such a way that when the ocean's tide was high, water would rush into the channel where the slaves were held. The water would then flow out, carrying feces and urine with it. The slaves' skin, rubbed raw by their overseers' whips and the manacles they wore, would bleed, stinging with the salt of the sea.

When I stared into that pit, I just could not comprehend the terrible cruelties this place had seen. I thought, too, about the reality that slavery didn't end in the nineteenth century. Millions of defenseless people are trafficked and abused all over the world today.

At this time, about half the population of Zanzibar lives below the poverty line. The average annual income is $250 U.S. More than one in every 10 children on the islands suffers from acute malnutrition. The child mortality rate is high. Life expectancy at birth is about 57 years. More than 99 percent of the population is Muslim, with a small Christian and indigenous minority. The indigenous people practice animism and witchcraft.

Years ago, a man named Simon was a witch doctor. Naked, he would sacrifice animals at night, and was well-known because of his connection with dark spirits. But he wanted more power. He heard voices telling him to sacrifice something more precious to him than a chicken or goat. So Simon ritualistically killed his 2-year-old son.

He sank deeper into the horror of the spirit world. His guilt and shame overwhelmed him. He had no hope.

Yet, at his bleakest moment of desperation, he went to a village where a pastor was telling people about Jesus Christ. He fell on his face and trusted Christ to remove his bloodguilt. He was baptized, studied the Bible, and is today a pastor who proclaims the Good News in areas still chained by the dark powers.

A distinct sense of darkness and oppression permeates this beautiful place. The last time I was there with a group from ICM, we went to went to Durajani, the central market in the city center. There were pyramids of fragrant spices, dates, pineapples, goat, shark, octopus, and many other exotic foods I could not even begin to identify.

When we travel on ICM trips, we strive to be culturally sensitive, but there was one woman in our group who did not have her upper arms covered. It was a modest shirt . . . so we were shocked when an angry Muslim man ran up to her outside a market stall, stuck her arm with a hypodermic needle, and then disappeared into the throng.

Our friend's arm went numb right away. She was terrified as the numbness spread. We immediately began praying for her and got her medical care. Eventually, she was okay. Shaken, but okay.

Radical Muslims have also tried to thwart our outreach on the islands. In some locations, they would come to church construction sites at night and steal the building supplies.

One young pastor we work with is a mighty man about 5 foot 4 inches tall, maybe 125 pounds. His wife is even smaller than he . . . but they are big and bold in their faith. Every time the walls were built for this pastor's church, Muslim extremists would come with hammers and picks, tear down the construction, and threaten the pastor's life.

The next day, the pastor and his team would commence work again. The Muslims kept coming. Finally, the diminutive pastor shouted at the bullies: "Fine! Go ahead! Kill me! Bury my body right here if you want, but this church WILL go up!"

They gave up.

And the church went up.

The Muslim-dominated government on Zanzibar expresses its distaste for Christian enterprises in subtler ways, making it extremely difficult for our partners to obtain permits for church buildings. So our brothers there have started applying to build "community centers." There are no crosses on top of these buildings. They are plain structures with side entrances. They function as a preschool during the week, and as a place of worship on Sundays. The quality of the child care and training there is so good that the Muslims have started sending their kids there—where they hear Bible stories and experience the love of Jesus.

CHAPTER 29

THE CRADLE ROCKS

"May God forgive the killers. We don't have hatred toward them. This is Christianity. God forgives the sinners. So shall we."

Fifi Shehata, whose father Maged
was one of 21 Egyptian Christians
beheaded by ISIS in Libya in 2015

When I think back to the Sunday school days of my childhood, it was easy to unconsciously assume that Christianity was a Western religion. Of course, I knew that Jesus lived in ancient Israel. I knew His followers fanned out from Jerusalem across the Middle East, and that the Good News eventually made its way from its origins to "the ends of the earth"—Europe and North America.

But most of the missionary stories I heard as a kid had to do with Americans going out to foreign lands. I heard little of indigenous Christian leaders in other nations. I didn't think much about the fact that Christianity was born 18 centuries before America even existed, and its cradle was the Middle East.

Take Iraq, home to ancient Babylon. Many scholars believe that Mesopotamia, with its conflux of rivers, was the site of the Garden of Eden. The great patriarch Abraham came from Ur; its ruins are located south of modern-day Baghdad. The Old Testament prophets Daniel, Jonah, and Ezekiel are buried in Iraq.

Think of Iran—ancient Persia—which plays such a dramatic role in the Old Testament tales, as do the lands of Assyria, Syria, and Lebanon. Think of Egypt, mysterious kingdom of the ancient Pharaohs, home to a Hebrew named Moses who led God's chosen people out of the Nile Delta, across the Red Sea, and into the Promised Land.

Jesus came to Egypt as an infant; His Gospel began to spread in Egypt after the day of Pentecost. The first churches were built there in the second century, and the new faith grew rapidly.

In the fourth century, when Emperor Constantine Christianized the Roman Empire, Christianity became the official religion of Egypt. In the seventh century, Arab Muslim armies overthrew Egypt's Byzantine rulers and conquered the country, bringing the new religion of Islam.

Islam generally did not take kindly to Christians and Jews. They were either slaughtered outright or offered a dubious choice: convert to Islam, pay the *jizya* tax—or be killed. Many fled for their lives. Egypt gradually became an

Arabic-speaking nation. Its ancient, original Coptic language was mostly lost, except for the rites of the Orthodox Coptic Church. By the end of the twelfth century, Egypt was mostly Muslim.

Today, Egypt is about 90 percent Muslim and 10 percent Christian, with a smattering of other belief systems. Friday is the Islamic holy day when offices are closed, Saturday is a part of the weekend, and Sunday is a normal business day.

In a way, that's hard for Americans to fathom. Every Egyptian citizen's religion is listed on his or her identity card. Even if a person is of nominal faith, he or she is categorized. There is no "none" box to check when you are asked about your religious allegiance. (Very few Egyptian identity cards read "Jewish." The country's Jewish population—about 100,000 in the mid-twentieth century—now numbers less than 12 people.)

Egypt's Christians face routine discrimination. They can't hold high political office. They are often hassled when it comes to getting jobs, driver's licenses, apartments, or building permits. A long-held culture of sectarianism is still in play.

One gets the impression, however, that while such prejudice is routine, it is little compared to the fears and violence of earlier times. Today's Egyptian Christians assert that Egypt has had more Christian martyrs than any other country on earth. Since the beginnings of their faith, they have been persecuted and killed by the forces of Rome, the Byzantines, the Ottomans, and extremist Muslims. Egyptian Christ-followers understand the cost of discipleship far more clearly than those of us who have grown up in societies where freedom of religion has been a given.

Take, for example, two modern news stories that brought Egyptian Christians to worldwide attention.

The first story played out during the summer of 2013. In the chaos after the fall of Egypt's then president, Mohammed Morsi, Muslim Brotherhood members and sympathizers burned police stations, government buildings, churches, Christian schools, and Christian-owned businesses all over Egypt.

In Al Nazla, a small village a few hours outside of Cairo, a large crowd burst through a church's gates, shouting slogans against Christians and calling for Egypt to become an Islamic state.

Various Catholic churches and monasteries were torched. The principal of a Catholic school in Bani Suef had assumed her school would be safe, as it educated equal numbers of Christians and Muslims. Not so. A mob broke into the school, stole computers and furniture, and set the building on fire. They knocked the cross off the street gate and replaced it with a black Islamist banner. They dragged the principal and two other nuns outside, parading them through the streets until a former teacher at the school, a Muslim, rescued them.

In various villages in Upper Egypt, Christian-owned businesses had already been marked with an ominous black X. Now they burned.

In Minya, a mob attacked and destroyed a Christian orphanage, leaving 200 children terrified and without shelter.

The Egyptian Bible Society had been quietly selling Bibles, books, and children's materials for 100 years in Egypt. At its bookshops in Minya and Assiut, attackers demolished the metal doors, broke the windows, and set everything on fire.

In Kerdasa, just outside Cairo, a mob broke down the gate of a church complex. They stole anything they could carry, then torched the rest and scrawled "Egypt is Islamic" on a wall.

The attacks, in dozens of locations, were conducted in a uniform way, with looting, burning, and destruction. Approximately 160 historic churches, businesses, homes, and cars owned by Christians were destroyed. In some places, Muslim men made a protective circle around churches, safeguarding those inside. Christians had done the same, protecting Muslims who were praying, during the upheaval of the Arab Spring of 2011.

Regardless of the perpetrators and their motivations, something remarkable happened in the smoldering ashes of Egypt's burned churches. In one town after another, banners were raised over the ruined buildings. Burned walls were scrawled with messages for the attackers.

The messages?

"We still love you!" And on the burned wall of one ruined orphanage: "You meant to hurt us, but we forgive you. God is love. Everything works out for good."[27]

In 2015, Ellen and I stood in the wreckage of one evangelical church that was burned back in the violent summer of 2013, and has not yet been rebuilt. My son, Matt, was with us. Matt has traveled all over the world with ICM and has seen many tough situations, but I could see the shock in his eyes as he took photographs of that ruined church. The cross had been wrenched from the chancel; the window grills and ceiling fans were bent from the heat of the flames. Charred Bibles lay in the ashes. We climbed up a still-standing stairway to the upstairs apartment where the pastor and his family had lived, stepping through debris to peek into the children's room. A Winnie the Pooh mural was still visible on the scorched wall.

The pastor and his family had been away at a Christian conference when the terrorists burned his church. We asked him how he had coped with the loss of his church and home. How had he dealt with such violation and hatred?

To him, the question seemed extraneous, and the root issue was simple: "What do we do in the face of evil?" he said to us through an interpreter. "We do what Jesus did. We *forgive.* Even after the destruction, we would still have fed the Muslim Brotherhood if they were hungry, or cared for them if they were sick."

At ICM, we take advantage of opportunities, whenever they appear, particularly in closed or difficult societies. Right now, we have a new opportunity to build worship centers, clinics, and Christian schools in Egypt. Since it's illegal in Egypt for Christians to gather for worship in private homes, church buildings are particularly important. We don't know how long this window will be open, but we and our Egyptian partners are accelerating our work there as much as we can.

Until recently, Egyptian law prohibited churches from repairing anything—a missing roof tile, a broken window—without the proper government form, a daunting document filled with mind-numbing pages of very small print. This form had to be signed, not just by some government functionary, but by the *president of Egypt.* So if a random church in Cairo needed a falling roof repaired, the members had to obtain, by some small miracle, the actual signature of the president of the entire nation. It was a reasonable bureaucratic strategy if the goal was to let churches in Egypt deteriorate.

One of our Egyptian partners remembers attending his dilapidated church as a teenager. The bathroom door had fallen off its crumbling hinges years before, but could not, by law, be repaired. His friends had to stand guard so he could use the facilities discreetly.

Now it is possible to get church building and renovation permits. We've built dozens of churches throughout Egypt through our key partner, a dynamo we'll call Dr. Sara. She is part of a large congregation in Cairo that we'll call the Neighborhood Church.

The church has been creative about building relationships with its Muslim neighbors. Members have distributed free wheelchairs to anyone in need in the community. They have a medical clinic, microfinance opportunities, and a preschool that serves the neighborhood. They organized a patriotic singing night, in which people of all faith traditions came to the church to sing songs about Egypt. They invited Muslims from the mosque down the street to a big breakfast in the church fellowship hall. About 200 people attended, and a few weeks later, the Muslims invited the Christians to the mosque for breakfast. The Neighborhood Church also organized a blood drive for a local blood bank. Christians and Muslims alike came to the church to donate, their blood mingling, as it were, for the good of their fellow citizens.

During the chaotic time when Muslim Brotherhood-inspired mobs were burning churches, gangs of angry young men would beat on the church doors during prayer meetings. They would scrawl threats on the outside walls. A Muslim policeman was assigned to protect the church, but one night the mob of attackers was too large and threatening. He, too, beat on the church doors, but in desperation, seeking sanctuary. The members took him in to protect him.

The church's Muslim friends called to warn members of other attacks by extremist hardliners. Then, as the Christians began to receive the breaking news that other churches all over Egypt were burning, they prayed about what to do. In the end, one of their pastors, Nabil, called one of the elders. "Tell the congregation to turn off the lights, lock the doors, and go," he said. "In the end, they can't stop us. We will rebuild the church if they burn it."

Pastor Nabil and his wife Deena were away at a previously planned youth retreat in Alexandria, on the Mediterranean Sea. They had 100 kids, ages 8 through 15, with them for several days of Bible study, fun, and fellowship. Then one of Nabil's elders received a threatening anonymous phone call.

"We are coming," the caller said. "We are coming to Alexandria, and we will burn your retreat center, with all those kids, to the ground."

The awful message was relayed to Nabil. He and Deena looked at the innocent faces of the happy kids around them. What could they do? They knew from other calls that the highways between Cairo and Alexandria were full of mobs, police, and chaos. They had heard of random shootings. They knew they needed to stay put. Their bus drivers had left, and transportation home was gone, anyway.

Nabil, Deena, and their team of 10 leaders started fasting and praying. They brought the children and young people in from outside. "We've had a change of plans!" they announced brightly. "We're going to play and have our meetings *inside*!" The kids looked around, bewildered. Why come inside when the delights of the sea were beckoning in the great outdoors?

The back of the retreat center faced the Mediterranean, with its front facing the highway from which any threat would come. As Nabil took stock, he couldn't help but think of a biblical parallel. Here they were, their backs to the sea, with no way of escape. He prayed that if the mobs came,

God would open the waters, just as He had for Moses 3,500 years earlier.

For 4 days, the adults prayed and the oblivious kids played. Nabil was constantly in touch with his church people in Cairo, who were trying to calm the kids' frantic parents. Finally, conditions on the highways improved enough that it seemed safe to move the kids back home. But there were no buses. A contact in Cairo finally made a connection in Alexandria, who procured transportation for the youth. There was a problem, however. Emblazoned on the sides of the two white buses, in huge black letters, were the words "Egyptian Christian Ministries." The word "Christian" seemed to leap right off the paint. If they encountered Islamist extremists on the highway, Nabil thought, it was like having huge targets on their buses: "Here we are! Christians!"

The youth leaders found some heavy white paper and masking tape. They covered over that offensive—and dangerous—word. *Christian*. After prayer, everyone climbed aboard. They closed the bus curtains and slowly made their way, through many checkpoints, down the highway to Cairo. It was too dangerous to rendezvous for a pickup with the kids' anxious parents at the church, so they went to a city park. There were shouts, hugs, rounds of applause, and tears. Many tears.

Nabil, Deena, and their own children made their way home. They tumbled into their beds, exhausted. "Those were such hard days, but blessed days," Nabil said later. "In the upheaval after the church burnings, some Christians left Egypt. Friends in the U.S. and Canada wanted us to emigrate. But we said no. We had discovered that we love our nation so much. We have much to do here. This is our time. Egypt is for Christ."

Our friends in Egypt tell us that by 2015, much of the violence of those anxious days in 2013 had abated. President

Abdel Fattah al-Sisi's government continued cracking down on terrorists. Former President Morsi and his colleagues, found guilty of treason, sat on Egypt's Death Row. Their Muslim Brotherhood sympathizers, forced underground, had blended into the general population, though emerging occasionally to execute bombings, assassinations, or other acts of terror.

Many Christians in Egypt refer to the turmoil of 2013 as "birth pangs," the pain necessary to get to a new beginning. They've passed through civil unrest, protests, upheaval and violence, to a new government that many hope, for the first time in decades, might just offer new opportunity and freedom.

It's still dangerous. Matt, Ellen, and I all raised our eyebrows a bit as we boarded our minibus to travel to villages in Upper Egypt. A nice man wearing a business suit and a semiautomatic submachine gun was now traveling with us, and as we hit the highway outside of Cairo, we found we also had a police escort of several vehicles in front of our bus, and several more vehicles behind us, all with sirens wailing.

As our noisy entourage arrived in a village in Upper Egypt, we weren't exactly stealth visitors. We walked into a crumbling church that will be rebuilt in cooperation with ICM. The pastor welcomed us. Several elders stood next to him, as well as the town's mayor, a Muslim man dressed in a flowing *jalabiya*. He and his fellow Muslims had contributed funds to build the church. They had seen the benefits a local group of Bible-believing Christians brings to a community. Schooling for kids in need. Medical help. Care for widows and orphans.

The pastor and the mayor grinned and gave us a message. "Tell our brothers and sisters in America," said the pastor, "that here in Egypt, we live in peace with our Muslim neighbors." The mayor nodded, and then invited us all to his home for coffee and pastries.

Sadly, in other villages, that peace has been broken. Muslim extremists have grabbed properties owned by Christian families for generations. In one village where ICM built a church, radicals kidnapped five Christian girls.

Our Egyptian partners tell us that such aggression by extremists has served to garner sympathy for Christians among moderate Muslims, the vast majority in Egypt. After the church burnings of 2013, "ordinary" Muslims were stunned by the cruelty of Muslim Brotherhood terrorists. They saw the hatred of the mob and its destruction of peace. Many determined to support their Christian neighbors. And some eventually came to churches with questions.

A young man I'll call Mo had read his Koran thoroughly. He wanted to believe the faith in which he'd been raised, but there were teachings he wondered about. "There were many things that I found intellectually lacking," he says. "I came to the point that I knew Islam was, in fact, not true. I just didn't know what *was* true."

Mo embarked on a spiritual search. Around the same time, he "coincidentally" met a family that had converted from Islam to Christianity. Like him, they had been faithfully seeking Allah. And their search for truth had led them to Jesus.

Like many Muslims, Mo struggled with the Christian claim that Jesus had died on the cross. Why would anyone worship a weak God, a God that would submit Himself to death? He had plenty of discussions, debates, and downright arguments with his new friends. They introduced him to Nada, a member of the young people's group at our ICM partner's church in Cairo.

Nada and the rest of the church welcomed Mo to their meetings. They hosted him for many meals and innumerable cups of coffee. Eventually, Mo says, "I knew Christianity was true. So I had to make a choice. Would I embrace the Truth? Or not?"

Drawn to the Kingdom by both its intellectual truth and its warmth and love, Mo determined to follow Jesus. He was baptized in 2014. A gifted musician, he became part of the church's dramatic outreaches. And when it was time to cast the singing role of Jesus in a play about the life of Christ, Mo got the part.

"I am part of the church family now," he told us. "And Jesus has made all the difference in my life. Having a relationship with a God who loves you is so much better than just knowing about a god that you only fear."

It's a great shame, at best, for Muslim families to acknowledge that their son or daughter has become a Christian. Sometimes it is cause for disinheritance or murder. Ellen asked Mo about his parents. What had they done in response to his conversion?

"Oh," he said, shrugging. "I should explain that I come from a very dysfunctional family. My parents divorced when I was young, my mom died a few years ago, and my dad and sister are always gone, always working or with their friends. They just aren't around, so they don't notice that I go to church five nights a week!"

Well, I thought, *perhaps this is one time to be grateful for a dysfunctional family!*

As I said earlier, two news stories focused the world's attention on Egyptian Christians. The church burnings of 2013 came first. Then, in early 2015, we all learned of ISIS's horrifying murders of 21 Egyptian believers on a bloody beach in Libya.

The young men were from Coptic families in poor villages in Upper Egypt. They had traveled to Libya to labor as migrant workers. One was saving money for a wedding. Another had been married only a short while. While in Libya, he got the news that his wife was pregnant. He sent almost everything he earned home. Another was earning money so he could afford a two-bedroom flat for his family. Another was funding his brother's university education.

On the night of December 28, 2014, the men were sleeping, along with migrant workers from other places. ISIS terrorists broke into their building. Some of the workers were able to hide; they later told the story of how the masked gunmen questioned who was Christian and who was Muslim. They took the Christians with them.

Upon hearing this awful news, the men's families back home in Egypt began to fast and pray. They knew ISIS. They knew the odious threat to their loved ones. And they prayed specifically that their husbands, brothers, and sons would stand fast. They prayed that when the decisive moment came, their men would not deny Christ.

We all know the rest of the story. The men were given the opportunity to recant. They did not. In a heavily orchestrated execution video, they were paraded in orange jumpsuits to the edge of the sea. Masked men in black pushed them down. The audio portion of the video picked up their voices. They didn't cry out. Instead, they whispered a name. *Yeshua. Jesus. Jesus.*

They were pushed down to their knees by their hooded oppressors. Many of them looked up toward heaven. The big knives came out. There was pain, blood, and darkness.

And then, the glories of His marvelous Light.

In Egypt, President Sisi declared a national day of mourning and executed airstrikes on ISIS targets. Churches filled with people praying for the families of those who had died so bravely. A week or two after the murders, Dr. Sara and several other leaders from Cairo's Neighborhood Church traveled to the village where 14 of the 21 men—all from one extended family—had lived.

"We were shocked," Dr. Sara says. "We had thought we were going to offer comfort and encouragement to the men's families. Instead, they encouraged *us*! They were so full of God's supernatural peace and the certainty that their men were with Him. Their faith challenged our faith. And they made us all the more determined to do whatever we can to share the powerful name of Jesus everywhere we can, in these dark times."

CHAPTER 30

WHAT GOD KNEW

"Sometimes we need to plunge our minds into the ocean of God's sovereignty. We need to feel the weight of it, like deep and heavy water pressing in against every pore, the deeper we go. A billion rivers of providence pour into this ocean.
". . . Sometimes we need to be reminded by God Himself that there are no limits to His rule. We need to hear from Him that He is sovereign over the whole world, and everything that happens in it. We need His own reminder that He is never helpless, never frustrated, never at a loss. We need His assurance that He reigns over ISIS, terrorism, Syria, Russia, China, India, Nigeria, France, Myanmar, Saudi Arabia, and the United States of America—every nation, every people, every language, every tribe, every chief, president, king, premier, prime minister, politician, great or small."
John Piper

When ICM began in the mid-1980s, my father had a big vision: reaching the world for Christ. He also had some clear first steps: building churches and disseminating the Mini Bible College. Still, Dad and his colleagues did not fully know where God would lead this ministry in the decades that would follow.

But God knew. And He knew exactly how He was positioning ICM to meet needs that were many years in the future.

The world is a far different place than it was in 1986, when ICM started. We are still all about nurturing believers and building worship centers—but now our partners are doing these things in extreme conditions.

As one of our field directors put it, when he used to go to North Africa and the Middle East a few years ago, the poverty was stunning. But now, he says, in addition to the physical needs, there is a tangible feeling of spreading evil. All over the world, forces of darkness march militantly to kill the Light. And just because the church in North America is not directly threatened, it would be heartless for us to ignore our brothers and sisters abroad, and foolish of us to ignore the potential peril for our own future.

The good news is that the darkness cannot extinguish the Light. We see that over and over in places where ICM works, places where we cannot even name our partners or their locations because doing so would jeopardize their security.

In one Southeast Asian country where the government is directly hostile to Christians, ICM pastors take turns going to jail. One has been in prison for 15 years; meanwhile, his wife has raised five children and kept their church going with such biblical faithfulness that it has grown to 1,000 people, and that congregation has planted 40 daughter churches.

Another pastor in this same country was out on his motorcycle inviting villagers to a Christmas service. He was stopped by government officials and a few henchmen, who stabbed him in the back and crushed his head with a boulder. His widow kept ministering in their church, which has now planted 30 more churches in that hostile area. Another Christian laywoman was sent to prison for her faith. The government found it in its best interest to release her when she led dozens of her fellow prisoners to Christ.

It is sadly common for our office to receive e-mails from our partners in tough areas, detailing violent situations. For example, a pastor and two laymen traveled to a church-building site in an African jungle to take photographs. They did so at night, so they wouldn't agitate people in the village who hated Christians. But, our partner reported, "I am told that after taking the photos, all hell befell on them when unknown people pounced on them, roughed and beat them badly, leaving them for dead. They also confiscated everything. Nobody came to their rescue."

The pastor and elders lay on the ground all night, groaning in pain. In the morning, passersby found them and took them to the hospital.

"I attribute all this," continued our partner, "to the past rebel insurgencies that disturbed the region for close to 25 years of war, that have left behind an unruly community. Another reason is that there are many witches who do not want to see a church thriving as souls coming to Christ denies them their following. Please pray for the quick recovery of the pastor and the other two members of the Bwobo church!"

Today, MBC is penetrating countries that are closed to Bible distribution, and Muslims are coming to know Jesus in places you would never dream. God is on the move.

Two believers were bringing 100 solar-powered units with MBC into a Muslim country. They had split the audio players into two suitcases, where the little units were crammed on top of each other, along with socks, shirts, and other clothing.

As our friends went through inspection, one of the buried players suddenly went off. You could hear a muffled voice from the suitcase, mysteriously preaching the Gospel in Arabic. There was no way to turn it off. Our friends looked at each other, prayed furiously, and smiled at the customs official. He either became temporarily deaf or beneficent. The suitcases made it through, and that audio player kept preaching the Gospel in the suitcase until our friend reached his home.

In Israel, we have worked with our partners to help build two worship centers for Messianic Jews. We just renovated another facility to shelter refugees—primarily women and children—from North Africa and the Middle East. Though they were Muslim, they had started showing up near one of our churches. Many had lost loved ones to ISIS; many of the women had been raped in their home country. They somehow knew that the church might be a place of healing and hope.

Because of the stress in that part of the world, some of our projects are unconventional. We recently completed a combination bomb shelter and youth outreach center. Teenagers come there to hear the Gospel; everyone comes there if missiles threaten from hostile nations.

One time I was with a partner from Israel while she was visiting the States, and she kept checking her cell phone. Then she apologized for appearing preoccupied. "I'm sorry," she said. "It's just that I know there's bombing going on in the neighborhood of our church, and I want to know if any of our members have been hurt or killed!"

I realized, sadly, that this situation was not unusual.

In one of the many Muslim countries that denigrate women and limit girls' education, ICM has built a beautiful school for young women. It's safe to say that part of that school's budget had to go to big fences, barbed wire, and security cameras. This was required by the government after extremists attacked young children in another local school.

In another challenging country, China, God opened doors for us to build many churches in one particular province. Many, many people came to know Jesus. It was a very fruitful season of opportunity, coinciding with the years before the Beijing Olympics. It looked like we'd be able to expand to other provinces . . . and then, due to some government changes, the door slammed shut.

We've always likened our work to the journeys of God's Old Testament people in the wilderness. God was with them in the presence of a big column, or pillar, of cloud to shade them by day, and a pillar of fire to light their campsite during the nights. When the pillar of cloud stopped, the people stopped. When it moved, they moved.[28]

ICM does the same. When God opens doors for us, particularly with hostile governments, we build churches like crazy. We only build where our partners can obtain government permission, and so if that door shuts, we stop.

As I write, we are waiting with great expectations to see when God opens China's door of opportunity again.

In this, we know He is at work. All we have to do is consider what happened in another communist country where the doors were closed to us for years.

ICM first started building churches in Cuba around 1997. As a stubborn communist holdout, Cuba was a political and ideological island, as well as a physical one. The United States had not recognized diplomatic relations with the government there since 1961.

Fidel Castro's iron hold on the island had meant disaster—in human terms—for Christians. They, like the government's political opponents, were harassed, injured, and imprisoned with impunity. Many followers of Christ left Cuba in a series of waves, starting after Castro's coup in 1959 and continuing into the 1980s.

In 1992, the Cuban government revised their constitution to identify the country as "secular" rather than "atheist." A few years later, Cubans were actually allowed to celebrate Christmas. And when my father first started traveling there, he discovered that ICM could make inroads in Cuba through our vibrant, godly partner, Bishop Ricardo Pereira Diaz of the Methodist Church.

During their first encounter, Bishop Ricardo and Dad flew by small plane all over Cuba. "As we traveled and visited people," Bishop Ricardo says today, "I felt like, without knowing it, we were completing a prophetic word God had given Joshua: 'I will give you every place you set your foot.' It was risky, but there are times in life when we have circumstances that are difficult, by human calculations. Are we going to obey God during those times? Or are we going to give in to fear?"

As ICM's partnership with the Cuban Christians grew, we built churches steadily. Dad and Burt would go to Cuba and ride to villages all over the island. Bishop Ricardo, typically Latin, free and passionate in his conversation, would zoom down dirt roads in an ancient, Russian-made car, talking the whole time and turning around to see Burt, who was crammed in the tiny backseat. "And that," Ricardo says today, poking fun at his old friend, "is how Brother Burt lost all his hair!"

In 2008, ICM was blocked from traveling to Cuba. The window of opportunity closed. We had built hundreds of churches, which, in turn, had planted new daughter congregations. We had helped train and disciple many pastors and lay leaders through the Mini Bible College. We could physically no longer go to Cuba . . . but we prayed for our brothers and sisters there with great hope.

In December 2015, after the United States re-established diplomatic relations with Cuba in July, Bishop Ricardo visited ICM's office in Virginia. He brought a Christmas message to our staff there: *Emmanuel . . . God with us!*

"God has been with us, unmistakably, over these many years in Cuba," Bishop Ricardo told us all, as passionate as ever. He had faced times of great difficulty. Thugs had stolen church supplies. He was the victim of a mysterious motorcycle "accident" when a government agent swerved into him, breaking a number of his bones. He spent time in prison. But he pressed on.

"People kept telling me, 'get out of Cuba!'" Ricardo said. "I said, 'NO! God is with us. And when He is with us, miracles happen.'"

Today, so many Cubans are coming to know Christ that mass baptisms are not uncommon. As many as 3,000 people will come on a Sunday afternoon to an appointed beach. Many bring guitars and other musical instruments. They sing, dance, and worship God while hundreds of people are baptized, one by one by one.

Recently, Ricardo was conducting a group baptism with 2,500 people present. Thirty government police were patrolling the beach, watching but doing little else. "It is illegal to do this," Ricardo shrugged. "But we do it anyway. And God is with us. What are the police going to do?

"The communists spent millions of dollars in their education system, teaching kids that there is no God," Ricardo went on. "But today, many young people are coming to faith in Jesus."

Older people are coming, too. Ricardo was preparing to baptize the last group of new believers during a recent service, when he looked up and saw a big, burly, middle-aged man before him. "I'm a colonel in the army," he told Ricardo. "I was formed by the communist system, told not to believe in God, that He did not exist.

"I'm a powerful military man," he went on, "with every kind of weapon available to me. Lots of people have to obey my commands."

The colonel dropped to his knees on the sand, bowing his head. Ricardo had to stoop to hear his words. "But before the Lord God, none of my weapons mean anything. My authority means nothing before His authority. So today, I want to be baptized!"

Ricardo dunked the military man, who wept with joy as he emerged from the water. Today, he is active in a local church, leading others to faith.

When ICM had to leave Cuba, we left our partners there with 212 churches. When Bishop Ricardo visited us in December 2015, his denomination alone had reached 402 churches and 700 preaching points, blanketing the island of Cuba. When we left, Ricardo's denomination had churches in 45 percent of Cuba's municipalities. Today, his denomination has penetrated every single municipality in his country. Ricardo's home church in Havana had

330 members when ICM had to pull back. Today, there are 3,200 members.

During his Christmas devotional at our office, Ricardo grinned and called my father to the front of the room. He clapped Dad on the back as he handed him a large, colorful map of Cuba, filled with dots representing each Cuban congregation. God had built His Church, and the gates of hell had not prevailed against it. Its explosive growth had happened through our indigenous, self-sustaining partners, in our absence.

I watched my father, tears in his eyes, hug his brother Ricardo. I was so grateful that he was seeing this fruit of what God had used him to begin. Then, characteristically, Dad turned back to the ICM staff. "This is how it's done, gang! It's all about our partners!"

Ricardo spoke up, echoing what Dad had said. "You came to us to build a bridge of faith in our most difficult years in Cuba," he concluded. "Now, I come to you, to encourage you, on that same bridge of faith. God is with us. And with Him, there are no limits!"

CHAPTER 31

THE BREATH OF HOPE

*"May God bless you with discomfort at easy answers,
half-truths and superficial relationships so that
you may live deep within your heart.
May God bless you with anger at injustice,
oppression and exploitation of people so that you
may work for justice, freedom and peace.
May God bless you with tears to shed for those who
suffer pain, rejection, hunger and war so that you may reach
out your hand to comfort them and to turn their pain into joy.
And may God bless you with enough foolishness
to believe that you can make a difference in the world
so that you can do what others claim cannot be done to bring
justice and kindness to all our children and the poor."*
A Franciscan Benediction

You read the Cambodian account of the God who hung on the cross in the foreword of this book. You know that the Cambodian people suffered horrifically during the dark days of communist dictator Pol Pot's vicious rule. Today, the most visible symbol of that suffering is Tuol Sleng prison.

When Pol Pot's Khmer Rouge took over Cambodia, they destroyed a quarter of the nation's population. They emptied the capital city, Phnom Penh. There, they took over a high school complex and turned it into a prison and interrogation center, one of many across the country. They called it S-21, or Tuol Sleng. From 1975 to 1979, between 17,000 and 20,000 people were imprisoned there.

Twelve emerged alive.

The victims in this horrific place were factory workers, soldiers, children, housewives, students, teachers, doctors, and priests. They were tortured into giving false confessions of crimes against the ruling regime. In the end, many of the torturers lost their lives there as well. Like the French Revolution's guillotine, Tuol Sleng's killing machine ended up devouring its own.

Invading Vietnamese soldiers found Tuol Sleng in 1979. The jailers there had mutilated and killed every prisoner they could before they escaped, just hours earlier. A combat photographer documented the soldiers' grisly discoveries.

Today, Tuol Sleng is a genocide museum. The original cells, torture chambers, and holding areas have been preserved. Like the Nazis, the Khmer Rouge obsessively documented their atrocities, and the prison walls show sobering black-and-white photographs of the thousands of people who passed through this place. A young mother stares resolutely into the camera, holding her tiny baby. A young man, bleeding from a head wound, fixes his eyes straight ahead. A little boy, his hands tied behind his back, does not know what has happened to him. A grandmother, her face a web of wrinkles, faces down her executioner. The photographs testify to human dignity, unique and precious, in the face of death.

I first walked the grim halls of Tuol Sleng many years ago. We had brought friends of the ministry to visit churches and orphanages that ICM had built in Cambodia. We'd met hundreds of children orphaned by AIDS, land mines, and other terrors, but who were now safe, secure, and joyful in their new relationships with Jesus.

We had also felt it important to show our guests Cambodia's sad historical context, so we had come to Tuol Sleng. I shivered, in spite of the jungle heat, as I looked at crude color paintings of some of the atrocities committed there. In one, soldiers laugh as they throw babies into the air and catch them on their bloody bayonets. In another, a prisoner weeps as he is tortured with electric shock. A shackled prisoner is waterboarded on a slanted wooden plank.

My oldest son was with me. Grant had been a little boy when Cambodian boys like him were murdered by their own people. I could not believe that these atrocities had happened—not in some barbaric, medieval period or in ancient history—but in our lifetime.

The last room we entered had an enormous map of Cambodia covering one wall. The map was made of 300 dry human skulls and leg bones, with the country's rivers marked in bloodred streams. The skulls were bashed, dented, and broken; their owners had died by blows to the head with iron bars and farm tools.

Even as I reflect on this horror today, all I can think of is the well-known Bible passage in Ezekiel 37.

The hand of the Lord was on me, and He brought me out by the Spirit of the Lord and set me in the middle of a valley; it was full of bones. . . . bones that were very dry. He asked me, "Son of man, can these bones live?"

I said, "Sovereign Lord, you alone know."

Then he said to me, "Prophesy to these bones and say to them, 'Dry bones, hear the word of the Lord! . . . I will make breath enter you, and you will come to life. . . . Then you will know that I am the Lord.'"

So I prophesied as I was commanded. And as I was prophesying, there was a noise, a rattling sound, and the bones came together, bone to bone. I looked, and tendons and flesh appeared on them and skin covered them, but there was no breath in them.

Then he said to me, "Prophesy . . . 'Come, breath, from the four winds and breathe into these slain, that they may live.'" So I prophesied as He commanded me, and breath entered them; they came to life and stood up on their feet—a vast army.

Then he said to me: "Son of man, these bones are the people of Israel. They say, 'Our bones are dried up and our hope is gone; we are cut off.' Therefore prophesy and say to them: 'This is what the Sovereign Lord says: My people, I am going to open your graves and bring you up from them . . . Then you, my people, will know that I am the Lord . . . I will put My Spirit in you and you will live . . . "[29]

I realize that Ezekiel's biblical revelation had to do with the Jews in exile and the historical period in which the prophet lived. But in light of the Gospel narrative of the entire Bible, Ezekiel's vision can also give great comfort to us. In today's broken world, we constantly deal with dry hearts, dead vision, and the lifeless remains of all we once hoped.

When my husband was diagnosed with cancer, and after it metastasized and he grew progressively weaker, I prayed constantly. I prayed for Bob, of course, and for all of us . . . "Oh, breathe on us, Breath of God! Animate us with Your Spirit, because apart from You, we can do nothing. Nothing."

And when Bob took his last breath on earth, I had the miraculous comfort that his next breath was in the presence of God.

That is the ultimate essence of hope for Christians. It also gives hope for this whole world. In today's fractured nations filled with murderous cruelty, there is hope because the Spirit of God is alive and well. He still brings life to dry bones.

It's not like the skulls in Cambodia or any other killing field have formed a vast army. But the spiritual void left by Pol Pot's slaughter created a fresh opportunity for the Gospel in that primarily Buddhist land. As in communist China, Vietnam, and Cuba, the number of Jesus-followers there is growing exponentially. As in Rwanda, another place stained by genocide, people are now studying God's Word, and the Holy Spirit is transforming them from the inside out. As in the former Soviet Union, or the most restricted areas of the Middle East, northern Africa, India, and in the refugee camps created by ISIS, God's Spirit is inexorably drawing men, women, and children to Jesus.

Chapter 32

Living Flat Out

"If we are to live 'flat out' and full of zeal to the end, the key is hope. . . . [the Apostle] Paul's knowledge of his hope in Christ had great invigorating, driving, and refreshing force. This is the key to aging with undiminished zeal."

John Piper

"We are sent into this world for a short time to say . . . through the joys and pains of our clock-time . . . the great 'yes' to the love that has been given to us and in so doing return to the One who sent us with that 'yes' engraved in our hearts. Our death thus becomes that moment of our return. But our death can be this only if our whole life has been a journey back to the One from whom we come and calls us the Beloved."

Henri Nouwen

In the beginning of this book, I told you about my love of God's connect-the-dot ways in our lives. When I look at the map of the world in ICM's office, full of all those dots that represent thousands of stories, I also think about how it all got started. Four decades ago, God connected my father and Pastor Dick Woodward. They stepped out in faith and obedience, with a passion for the Great Commission and a willingness to pour out their lives to serve God and other people. They didn't know what would happen, but they trusted God, and the rest is His story.

I think of my own life over the past few decades. When my husband was battling cancer, when my identity and purpose were challenged, when I didn't know what would happen with my sons or their futures, let alone my own . . . during it all, God was connecting random dots to create an image of unlikely hope and peace. For me, it came as a whisper to my soul. *"I am God. I love you. I love the whole world. I love you so much that I sent my only Son to give His life so you could live forever. Trust me!"*

A few years ago, I was in a church in Africa. As I looked at the beautiful, joyous faces of the congregation, I realized that God had brought me full circle, back to my childhood desire to serve in Africa. My dreams *did* come true. Certainly not in the way I had envisioned, but God has made it possible for me to travel all over the world, to understand degrees of need I never knew existed, and to see healing, exuberant joy, indescribable peace, and His presence in places you would least expect.

The challenges I faced along the way are not unusual. For all of us, life is unpredictable. It turns in directions we do not want. People we love die too soon. Children go in directions we desperately hoped they would not. We lose our job, our savings, or our home. People betray us. Couples face years of infertility. Spouses get dementia.

My mom and dad celebrated 72 years of marriage in 2015. I consider it an enormous blessing to have both my parents still alive. I know this is uncommon at my age, and I don't take this gift for granted.

But this longevity has not come unscathed.

My family started noticing my mother's memory loss around the same time my husband's cancer had spread. We excused Mom's occasional vagueness and hoped for the best, but Christmas 2003 was a turning point.

My parents loved having the extended family gather at their home for a bountiful dinner on the day after Christmas. Mom had always been the planner, the cook, the one who made Christmas festive for the rest of us. She decorated every inch of her home. She packed stockings full of thoughtful gifts. She carefully placed beautifully wrapped packages around the tree. The house smelled of turkey, freshly baked rolls, and Christmas candles.

In 2003, when we arrived at our childhood home, the turkey stuffing was still in Pepperidge Farm packages. The green beans were in cans. The stockings were empty. Dad had gone out to the store, trying to provide what only Mom could do.

Mom's memory issues had been progressing long before that Christmas, but we had been slow to admit the change.

Almost 13 years later, I marvel that my parents are still alive, still joyously celebrating life. Love prevails, even during those moments when the disease takes over, and my mother is no longer the woman my father knows so well. I've admired my dad's kind patience, his willingness to shop, cook, and serve her. I have seen my sisters choose her outfits carefully so she remains the gracious, lovely woman she has always been. Our family's assignment is to love and honor her until God calls her home. She grows more beautiful every day.

My father didn't want to have a big party to celebrate their landmark seventieth wedding anniversary. Just our immediate family joined them for dinner in the formal dining room of the Williamsburg Inn. My sister, Cindy, brought the scrapbook my mother had put together during her engagement and wedding. Typical of the time, the book contained newspaper clippings describing each bridal shower and wedding event in detail. The newspaper even listed every song that had been played at the wedding reception.

The Williamsburg Inn's restaurant pianist came over to our table and asked what we were celebrating. We showed him the playlist of wedding songs. He went straight to his piano to play my parents' favorite, and they got up to dance. The rest of us watched in tears as they waltzed gracefully, so old yet forever young, to the song that had celebrated their wedding in 1943.

As anyone who has dealt with memory loss in a loved one can tell you, it can cruelly steal so much. But on this anniversary night, I saw how, as the Bible says, love never fails . . . and that God can turn mourning into dancing.

My parents' legacy is clear to me as I think of the hundreds of thousands of lives they've touched for Jesus through ICM, and the character they've imprinted on our family and the generations that follow.

Sometimes I wonder: what legacy will I leave? It's tempting for all of us to live life's quick decades in an acquisitive,

Christianized version of the American dream, and to settle for a life that may be long on résumé accomplishments, but short on eternal impact. It's easy to waste time obsessing over idols. These aren't the literal idols made of wood or plastic that I've seen in primitive villages in India or Africa. They are much subtler and more sophisticated—and therefore, much deadlier.

A good friend gave me a great example of this. He's a successful businessman who inherited an ornate, historic Virginia hillside mansion. Its acreage and buildings are worth millions of dollars. Rare, custom antiques fill the home. It is gorgeous.

My friend found, however, that his pleasure about owning this masterpiece began to fade as he discovered that the home was beginning to own him. He thought about it constantly. He worried about its upkeep, its safety, its worth.

Eventually, he told me that he'd become like Gollum in *Lord of the Rings*, the character who is fatally obsessed with the Ring of Power, which he calls his "Precious."

"I don't want this property to become my Precious!" my friend told me wryly.

So he put it up for sale, and ever since, he has been free to focus on heavenly mansions rather than earthly ones.

I don't own any mansions on a hill, but my friend's experience made me wonder, what do I hold too tightly, making me miss the miracles of God's provision? I want to run life's race unimpeded by "stuff," whether physical possessions or mental baggage.

In this, I am forever grateful to the sisters and brothers I've met through ICM's ministry in poor countries. Their faith challenges my own, as they depend on God for everything, even when life is cruel and makes no sense. They have shown me that trusting God alone can bring life when all else seems dead. As a pastor from a violent African nation told me, "The enemy uses all his weapons to bring discouragement, but we are not people who throw in the towel. We are holding onto God's promises and going all the way to the end."

Learning to trust God in the crossroads of my life has drawn me down a path richer and more wondrous than I could have imagined. The journey has been unexpected, but extraordinary, and I trust God's promise that He will continue to do more than I ever envisioned, in my own journey and through the ministry of ICM. While the challenges of our world today are great, there is no doubt that God's Spirit is moving powerfully across the nations. We also know that "no eye has seen, no ear has heard, no mind has conceived, what God has prepared for those who love Him."[30]

So there is hope. Always hope.

May the God of hope fill you with all joy and peace
as you trust in Him, so that you may overflow with hope
by the power of the Holy Spirit.
Romans 15:13

ENDNOTES

Please note that, due to security reasons, we have changed some of the names in this book.

1. Revelation 7:9–10.

2. http://www.un.org/en/globalissues/briefingpapers/food/vitalstats.shtml

3. http://utmost.org/are-you-fresh-for-everything/

4. Lettie B. Cowman, *Streams in the Desert*, April 16, Zondervan, 2016.

5. John Baillie, *A Diary of Private Prayer*, Touchstone, 1996.

6. http://utmost.org/classic/diffusiveness-of-life-classic/

7. Psalm 23:4, *The Message*.

8. See Henry Blackaby, Richard Blackaby, Claude King, *Experiencing God*, revised and expanded edition, B&H Books, 2008, and Henry Blackaby and Claude King, *Experiencing God Workbook: Knowing and Doing the Will of God*, Lifeway Christian Resources, 1990. Henry Blackaby's teaching is based on seven essential principles:

> *God is always at work around you.*
> *God pursues a continuing love relationship with you that is real and personal.*
> *God invites you to become involved with Him in His work.*

God speaks by the Holy Spirit through the Bible, prayer, circumstances, and the church to reveal Himself, His purposes, and His ways.

God's invitation for you to work with Him always leads you to a crisis of belief that requires faith and action.

You must make major adjustments in your life to join God in what He is doing.

You come to know God by experience as you obey Him and He accomplishes His work through you.

9. See 1 Peter 2:5.

10. http://www.newworldencyclopedia.org/entry/William_Temple

11. 2 Corinthians 12:9–11.

12. http://www.ghrc-usa.org/wp-content/uploads/2012/01/ThreethousandandCountingAReportonViolenceAgainstWomeninGuatemala1.pdf, and International Justice Mission, "Study of the Guatemalan Criminal Justice System, Cases of Sexual Violence against Children and Adolescents," 2013.

13. See Acts 8:26–40.

14. Barbara Brown Taylor, *An Altar in the World: A Geography of Faith*, HarperOne, 2010.

15. This account is adapted from Chapter 31 of Ellen Vaughn's book *Time Peace*, Zondervan, 2007.

16. This account is from James Hefley, *By Life or By Death*, Zondervan, 1969.

17. There is much that is not known about the events at Ban Me Thuot that day. This account is drawn from Marie Ziemer's descriptions, Ellen Vaughn's conversations with Admiral Tim Ziemer, son of Bob and Marie, James Hefley's *By Life or By Death,* and various POW Web sites. Marie passed away in September 2012 at the age of 93.

18. "Anywhere With Jesus," lyrics by Jessie Brown Pounds, music by Daniel Brink Towner.

19. Galatians 6:17.

20. According to Michael Benge, a U.S. AID worker who was taken prisoner along with Betty Olsen and Hank Blood, the Viet Cong constantly

moved their captives. Living in the jungle, the three Americans suffered from diarrhea, infections, leeches, and ulcerated sores. Hank Blood died of pneumonia in July 1968; Mike and Betty buried him along the jungle trail, and Betty conducted a funeral service. Mike credits Betty with keeping him alive after he contracted malaria that summer, but Betty died of malnutrition and dysentery in late September of '68. Mike Benge survived his Viet Cong captivity and was released in March 1973. He lives in Northern Virginia, where Ellen Vaughn interviewed him in 2014.

21. https://www.cmalliance.org/alife/in-the-line-of-fire/

22. Ibid.

23. Vietnamese proper names and surnames are written, accented, and identified differently from North American usage. For the purposes of this book, we're using American ways of identifying names.

24. In these descriptions, as elsewhere, we are indebted to Denise Chong's excellent book, *The Girl in the Picture: The Story of Kim Phuc, the Photograph, and the Vietnam War*, Penguin Books, New York, 1999.

25. http://www.commissionstories.com/asia/stories/view/temple-prostitution-still-alive-in-india

26. http://www.houseofrefuge-india.org/sleeping_goddess.html

27. Some of this material is drawn from *Mama Maggie*, by Marty Makary and Ellen Vaughn, Tyndale, 2015.

28. See Exodus 13:20–22 and 40:34–38.

29. See Ezekiel 37:1–14.

30. 1 Corinthians 2:9.

International Cooperating Ministries (ICM) is a nonprofit ministry propelled by the desire to see the Church advanced and supported across the globe. ICM works through strategic indigenous partnerships in a highly leveraged system for accomplishing Church growth work. With paid staff only in the U.S., administrative costs are supported by private foundations, allowing every designated dollar to be applied in total to the cost of projects. ICM joins with partners from all varieties of evangelical churches, resulting in a rich and dynamic body of believers. ICM is at the forefront of the Great Commission. With a plan by 2020 to build 10,000 churches, plant 50,000 daughter congregations, establish 100,000 Bible study groups, and equip 1 million evangelists, ICM is taking on the task of reaching the world for Christ. Join with ICM and be a part of building churches and distributing Bible study materials around the world!

For more information, visit www.icm.org or call 1-800-999-3892. ICM is located at 1901 N. Armistead Avenue in Hampton, Virginia 23666-4311.

WITH GRATITUDE

JANICE ALLEN

Many people have made this book possible.

I would first and foremost like to express my deep gratitude to Ellen Vaughn, whose creativity, insight, and quirky sense of humor have made this entire project an exciting journey. Her patience and friendship have been a welcome gift and enriched my life.

I am especially grateful to my family:

Bob, for everything he taught me about what it means to truly love another person, for the laughter, tears, and rich memories.

My parents, Dois and Shirley Rosser, who taught me how to live with strength, kindness, grace, and an unwavering certainty about the faithfulness of God.

My incredible sons, Grant, Matt, and Connor. Thank you for your encouragement and support to follow a new path. You have brought me unlimited joy from the minute you were born, and I am so grateful for the three gifted young women God has brought into your lives . . . Kate, Adrienne, and Paige.

My precious sisters, Pam and Cindy. I cannot imagine life without you.

I am grateful for the "band of sisters" (Sally, Marci, Carolyn, Elizabeth, Michelle, Jo, Terri, Annhorner, and Randee) who faithfully prayed and cared for me on days when the journey was hard. Your support and friendship have been more precious than gold.

Thank you to the group of visionary leaders on the ICM Women's Initiative Steering Committee (Janet Ward, Nancy, Saundra, Ellen, Kim, and Pat), who have inspired me more than they will ever know. I am especially grateful for my faithful mentor, Saundra Winge. Thank you for pouring "pearls" into my life to guide me and remind me of God's promises. Thank you for your prayers down the home stretch of the book.

I am deeply grateful to Dr. Jim and Heather Gills for their faithful prayers, guidance, and generous support they have given to me and to ICM.

Very special thanks to the entire ICM team, especially Geof, Burt, Jan, Don, and Lisa. It is an honor and blessing to co-labor with you to advance Christ's Kingdom around the world!

This project was brought to life by the stories of courageous men and women of faith I have met along this journey—you have inspired me, humbled me, blessed me, and enriched my life immeasurably.

There are no words to describe my overwhelming gratitude to my Lord and Savior Jesus Christ, who loves me unconditionally and has graciously and faithfully met me at each crossroad. He is my anchor, my only hope in this life and in the life to come.

ELLEN VAUGHN

Ironically, around the same time Janice and I started working on this book, delving into the story of her husband's terrible cancer, my own husband received a dire diagnosis. Lee did not have ocular melanoma, like Bob Allen. But, like Bob's, my husband's cancer was rare, malignant, and aggressive. Lee had a tumor growing in his sinuses that extended into his brain. It would kill him unless we acted quickly.

I can't imagine a more supportive friend and colleague than Janice during the course of Lee's surgeries, extensive radiation, chemotherapy, and slow recovery! This book was put on hold for more than a year. During that time, God not only gave Lee a gracious reprieve, He also did amazing new things through ICM's ministry. By the time Janice and I were able to return to the writing process, the book's focus had grown. So had we, and I believe this book is richer for it.

Thank you, Dois Rosser, for introducing me to ICM back in 2000. Dois has been a father figure to me for years, though I'm just not as cool as his three real daughters. I'm so grateful to everyone in the ICM family who made this book possible by consenting to interviews, hosting me in foreign countries, and plying me with really good coffee. I thank all those who reviewed the manuscript, corrected its errors, and made suggestions, including Lee and Laura and Jim Warren.

I'm full of gratitude for the many friends who supported our family—Lee, me, Emily, Haley, and Walker—through the complicated course of Lee's cancer journey, and at the same time, prayed for the creation of this book: Patti Bryce, my sisters Gloria and Gail, Norma Vaughn, Cameron Malloy, the CHEEKS, HMS, Supper Club, our couples' small group, ICM staff, Women's Initiative folks, and so many other dear sisters and brothers who tenderly cared for us at our darkest hours and celebrated with us in our sweetest joys. Special thanks to the prayer group that George and Connie Stewart pulled together!

I'm so grateful for my fellow board members at ICM, for Geof Stiff and the executive leadership, and for the lifelong friends I've made on some pretty crazy vision trips. Thank you so much to Burt Reed and the other field directors, and to ICM's partners, the heroes in the field.

Most of all, I thank God for showing me, through ICM, a window of what He is doing in the world today. I am forever grateful for the believers I've met who are suffering persecution, discrimination, and deprivation, and I am privileged to tell some of their stories. Their relentless good humor, hope, and robust faith have forever strengthened my own.